WHO ARE YOU?

The Book of Tests for Getting to Know Who You Are and How You Function

Sidney Lecker, M.D.

A FIRESIDE BOOK

published by Simon and Schuster
NEW YORK

Acknowledgment

My gratitude to Professor R. O. Pihl and Dr. Amos Zeichner of McGill University for creating many of the tests contained in this book.

A Fireside Book
Published by Simon and Schuster
A Division of Gulf & Western Corporation
Simon & Schuster Building
Rockefeller Center
1230 Avenue of the Americas
New York, New York 10020

Manufactured in the United States of America

1 2 3 4 5 6 7 8 9 10

Library of Congress Cataloging in Publication Data
Lecker, Sidney.
Who are you?
(A Fireside book)
1. Personality tests. 2. Self-evaluation—Testing. I. Title.
BF698.5.L42 155.2′83 79-12836

ISBN 0-671-24750-6

Are You the Type of Person Who Can Benefit by Reading This Book? Take This Test and Find Out.

Circle One Letter for Each Test Item

A = strongly agree
a = mildly agree
d = mildly disagree
D = strongly disagree

---

(1) Sometimes the more you know about a problem concerning emotions the worse the problem gets.

A (a) d D

(2) A child should be taught the lesson of the saying "Curiosity killed the cat."

A a (d) D

(3) Talking to friends about problems only makes things worse. It's better not to wash your dirty linen in public.

A (a) d D

(4) I am the type of person who is dedicated to improving the lives of those around me even at my own expense.

(A) a d D

(5) My parents or the dominant adult in my upbringing was prone to give commands without explanations.

A (a) d D

(6) I respect people who stand on their own two feet and never bother people around them for advice. Nobody really cares about someone else's problems anyway.

A (a) d D

(7) A leader who permits subordinates too much freedom usually runs into trouble.

A a (d) D

(8) If I were a politician I would pass more laws against things like indecent movies and books, perverse sexual habits, and public nudity.

A a (d) D

(9) The ideal spouse is someone who has a strong sense of duty above all other traits.

A (a) d D

(10) Religion serves an important purpose for people by reminding them to curb repugnant urges.

A a (d) D

Scoring:

A = minus 2   a = minus 1   d = plus 1   D = plus 2

If you scored 10 or more, read this book — you will benefit by it. If you scored less than 10, don't waste your time.

CONTENTS

Why Learn About Tests?

A test is simply a more intelligent way of asking an important question for which you need an answer.

Should we marry? Are we compatible?

Are we psychologically ready to have a child?

Why am I so frustrated at work?

Why do I get depressed? Am I neurotic?

I wonder how my child's intelligence and personality are shaping up?

My girl friend says I'm great in bed. Is she just flattering me or am I really a talented lover?

Am I the type that is prone to heart attacks? If so, I'd like to know so that I can change my ways and prolong my life.

When I consult a doctor or lawyer, I'm really buying a blind article. Is there any way I can rate the skills of these expensive professionals?

Every day you are faced with some minor or major decisions in life. In order to guide yourself to a beneficial course of action you carry on an internal dialogue with yourself. You ask yourself questions about *who you are* and how you might best fulfill your needs. All too often, you don't spend enough time elaborating on the question. Your mind is impatient for an answer that will permit a course of action toward a solution. You rush past the question and give yourself a shoot-from-the-hip answer.

"Should we marry? Of course. We're in love, aren't we?" You convince yourself to move ahead quickly so as to decrease the frustration arising from your uncertainty. Years later, both of you say, "Why were we in such a damned hurry to get married? What a mistake!"

If you want *quick solutions*, ask slow, carefully planned questions.
If you ask hurried, abbreviated questions, the solutions may be long, painful, and costly.
A test is a system of questions that prepares you for an effective solution to a problem. It is a detailed and expanded version of the original question you had in mind with extensions into all important areas that might affect the outcome of your course of action.

"Should we get married?" you ask. "Okay, let's put this issue to a test. What are your important needs for now and in the foreseeable future? What are my needs? How will marriage promote our interests? How much compromise will it involve? How will I react to giving up some of my privacy and autonomy? What about you?

By exploring the question in this way, the couple is beginning to tap into important areas of their personalities, aspirations, and values. They are preparing the way for an intelligent solution. Further elaboration of the original question is exactly what a good test is all about. If you learn how to construct appropriate tests for each problem you face, you will find accurate and helpful answers more easily.

Can I Rely on Tests?

Do you remember the swimming test you had at camp? The lifeguard said, "If you swim thirty lengths of the pool, you can take out a canoe on your own." He constructed a test of swimming proficiency to measure whether you would have the stamina to swim to shore if the canoe capsized. Could you and he rely on that test? The answer is, "Only under certain conditions." What if a storm made the water extremely rough with a strong current going against you? What if your energy level was low because of the flu you were incubating? Could you reach shore under those circumstances? Probably not. However, under most predictable circumstances, swimming thirty laps would ensure that you were a strong enough swimmer to make it to shore.

Any test is really a limited sample of attitudes or behavior under specified conditions. It can predict your future performance, but not under all conceivable conditions. Despite this limitation, it was far better for the lifeguard to make sure your could swim thirty laps than to simply ask, "Do you think you will be able to reach shore if the canoe capsizes?" and then take your word for it that you could.

Similarly, if you take a personality test and the results indicate that you tend to be overly serious, ambitious, and organized and consequently may be a cardiac risk, that doesn't mean you will act overly serious in an amusement park or when having a drink with friends. Tests give you an accurate idea of tendencies. They are not infallible predictors, but they are far better than hurried guesses about the future.

Are Tests Always Important?

Yes! Here is one example of a test that everyone should take before owning a dog:

	Yes	No

(1) If a burglar broke into your house, would you lay down your life to protect your dog?

(2) If *The New York Times* put out a Canine Edition, would you get a subscription for your dog?

(3) Do you believe that the man who invented doggie galoshes should be awarded the Nobel Prize?

(4) Are dogs more emotionally sensitive than most people?

(5) Should they impose the death penalty for dog-napping?

Scoring:

If you answered No once, you've failed this test. Buy yourself a new color TV and let someone else have the joy of bringing up a dog.

How Can Tests Help Me?

Any time there is a decision to make, you need to know as many facts as possible beforehand. Knowing what makes you tick is essential. You assess the situation confronting you, and if you know yourself well enough, you will be prepared to act effectively. For example, if you are offered a job you may well wonder whether you will be suited for it. An aptitude test (such as the type described in Chapter Four) that reveals your talents and potential skills combined with a personality profile (as in Chapter Three) will give you excellent information as to whether you are suited for the job by disposition and abilities.

Some tests are useful in helping you understand your relationship with people. Suppose you and your spouse are faced with behavior problems in your child. You ask yourselves, "Where are we going wrong?" Because of the painful nature of the problem and the parental tendency to minimize differences of opinion and present the children with a "united front," significant differences in child-rearing approaches often go unrecognized and undiscussed. Consequently, the parents fight an invisible tug-of-war, each presenting the child with a different set of rules, and the child begins to act up out of confusion and frustation.

A test that could expose these differences in child-rearing styles would serve the parents well in enabling them to pinpoint areas of hidden conflict and to effectively resolve the irritating issues.

In the following test, you and your spouse should answer all the questions separately, not revealing your responses until after you have both completed the entire questionnaire. Then compare answers and note those on which you differed. These areas will provide useful guidance in resolving differences in child-rearing approaches.

These are some questions about family life and children. Read each of the statements below and then rate them as follows, circling the appropriate letter.

A = strongly agree   a = mildly agree   d = mildly disagree   D = strongly disagree

There are no right or wrong answers, so answer according to your own opinion. Please work as quickly as possible.

(1)	Children should be allowed to disagree with their parents if they feel their own ideas are better.	A a d D
(2)	Playing too much with a child will spoil him.	A a d D
(3)	A good mother should shelter her child from life's little difficulties.	A a d D
(4)	A child should not plan to enter any occupation that his parents do not approve of.	A a d D
(5)	The home is the only thing that matters to a good mother.	A a d D
(6)	Too much affection will make a child a "softie."	A a d D
(7)	A watchful mother can protect her child from any accidents.	A a d D

(8) It is frequently necessary to drive the mischief out of a child before he will behave.   A a d D

(9) Children should realize how much parents have to give up for them.   A a d D

(10) All young mothers are afraid of their awkwardness in handling the baby.   A a d D

(11) If children are quiet for a little while a mother should immediately find out what they are thinking about.   A a d D

(12) People who think they can get along in marriage without arguments just don't know the facts.   A a d D

(13) A mother has to suffer much and say little.   A a d D

(14) A child will be grateful later on for strict training.   A a d D

(15) Children will get on any woman's nerves if she has to be with them all day.   A a d D

(16) When the father punishes a child for no good reason the mother should take the child's side.   A a d D

(17) It's best for the child if he never gets started wondering whether his mother's views are right.   A a d D

(18) More parents should teach their children to have unquestioning loyalty to them.   A a d D

(19) A child should be taught to avoid fighting no matter what happens.   A a d D

(20) Parents should sacrifice everything for their children.   A a d D

(21) For a woman one of the worst things about taking care of a home is the feeling she can't get out.   A a d D

(22) A mother should make it her business to know everything her children are feeling at all times.   A a d D

(23) Parents should adjust to the children to some extent, rather than always expecting the children to adjust to them.   A a d D

(24) There are so many things a child has to learn in life there is no excuse for him sitting around with time on his hands.   A a d D

(25) A parent must never make mistakes in front of the child.   A a d D

(26) If you let children talk about their troubles they end up complaining even more.   A a d D

(27) Mothers would do their job better with the children if fathers were more kind.   A a d D

(28)   Most children are toilet-trained by fifteen months of age.   A   a   d   D

(29)   A young child should be protected from hearing about sex.   A   a   d   D

(30)   Children should not annoy parents with their unimportant problems.   A   a   d   D

(31)   Children and husbands do better when the mother is strong enough to settle most of the problems.   A   a   d   D

(32)   A child should never keep a secret from his parents.   A   a   d   D

(33)   Children who take part in sex play become sex criminals when they grow up.   A   a   d   D

(34)   Children would be happier and better behaved if parents showed an interest in their affairs.   A   a   d   D

(35)   A devoted mother has no time for a social life.   A   a   d   D

(36)   The sooner a child learns to walk, the better he's growing up.   A   a   d   D

(37)   Children should be taken to and from school until the age of eight just to make sure there are no accidents.   A   a   d   D

(38)   Taking care of a small baby is something that no woman should be expected to do all by herself.   A   a   d   D

If, after discussing the areas where you and your spouse disagree, some differences still remain unresolved, you can at least recognize the problem areas and not let your children play "both ends against the middle." You can decide whose influence is more significant for the child at this point in his or her development and allow that parent's point of view to prevail.

Can I Learn to Develop My Own Tests for Important Areas in My Life?

Developing a test is not a complicated procedure. There are different basic test structures that you can employ, depending on the problem to be solved. Throughout this book, numerous tests are explained and demonstrated. The last chapter outlines a program by which you can develop tailor-made tests for many purposes. Let's examine one test system we use in changing problem behavior at the Stress Control Center in New York.

Many executives who come to our center are under destructive levels of stress. Their lives have become wrapped up in their jobs, and over the years both their work and family satisfactions begin to wane. In these cases we ask the person to construct a "sociogram" of his relationships with people. Consider the sociogram of Bill, a troubled executive:

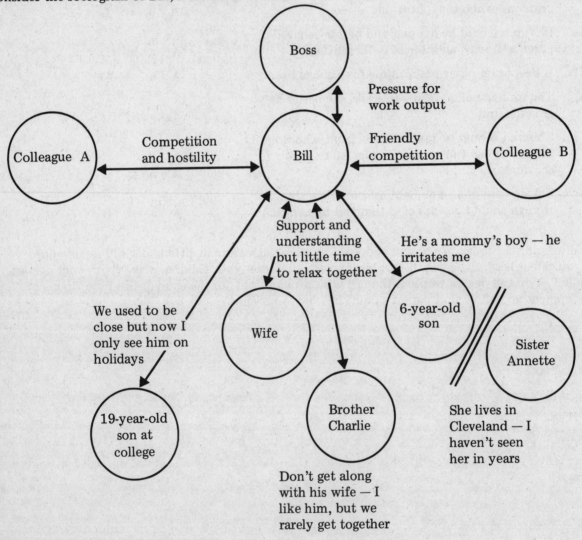

When Bill sketched out this diagram of his social relationships it struck him right away that he didn't have a single consistent satisfying relationship in his life. "No wonder I find everything so irritating and distasteful," he said. "I've let all my important relationships drift into limbo. Not one single person or friend can be an ego-booster for me. I'm distant from everyone."

Bill was then asked to sketch out an improved pattern of relationships that he could feasibly establish in the near future. He drew this:

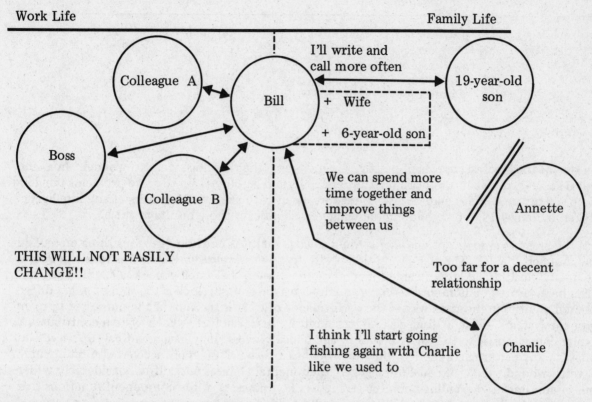

The sociogram is a good test for diagnosing social relationships, their sources of gratification and frustration. Bill was able to shift his relations with his family quite easily as soon as he became aware that therein existed a potential for satisfaction lying dormant because of his pre-occupation with his work. Interestingly enough, as soon as he felt more comfortable and gratified in his home life, he was more successful in dealing with the job demands and competition from his colleagues.

You must learn *how to ask the questions* that can lead to solutions that will influence your life in beneficial ways.

You must learn *how to analyze* the results of the explorations you undertake in attempting to find solutions to your life problems.

You must *have goals* for change and know how to implement them.

Your only tool for achieving success is yourself. **Who Are You?** is the central question of your existence.

If you know your potentialities, you will use them.

If you know your weaknesses, you will overcome them or at least avoid being trapped by them.

If you know how you interact with others, you will learn how to be a more effective and thus contented person.

Knowing the methods of test construction and analysis is a key to intelligent behavior, accurate prediction, and fruitful planning. **Who Are You? The Book of Tests** is your source of this vital knowledge.

1 How Good Are Your Smarts?

By far one of the greatest sources of prestige for humans is their intelligence. No wonder. In a technological society, the ability to learn difficult concepts and employ them to solve problems is a good predictor of future security and success. Hence we await with anxiety the results of any intelligence test taken by ourselves or our children, knowing how significant those results might be.

One of the greatest misconceptions about intelligence is that it is one homogeneous thing measurable by one number, the IQ. Through promotion of IQ testing and releasing IQ scores to the public, we in the mental health field are to blame for creating the illusion that intelligence is a simple quantity that can be measured in numerical terms. Actually a person's intelligence is the sum of many different mental abilities in the same way as the performance of a car is the sum of the output of its many component systems — engine displacement, carburetion, suspension etc. Each system contributes a particular characteristic to the car's operation, and hence two cars may have identical top speeds but one may handle better in cornering while the other has a better 0-60 mph acceleration rate. Similarly, with two individuals of equal intelligence, their mental abilities may differ considerably under various circumstances depending upon the strengths or weaknesses of the component functions that make up total intelligence. In this chapter you will be able to test six major constituents of intelligence:

(1) Abstraction: the ability that helps you figure out complex problems dealing with intangibles, a basic reasoning skill essential to all fields of work.

(2) Visual organization: the skill of mental categorization and analysis by visual means, essential to mathematicians, architects and engineers, surgeons, and in many other professions.

(3) Memory: the critical component of so many vocations, especially law, medicine, and many fields of business.

(4) General knowledge: the sign of a well-read and broadly experienced individual.

(5) Incidental learning: a particular trait of the highly successful whose minds seize on every opportunity for learning.

(6) Attention: a trait essential for success in many critical occupations such as driving a car, piloting an airplane, analyzing complicated financial statements, or typing quickly and efficiently.

As you take these tests you should be precise in your answers but avoid wasting time since speed combined with accuracy improves your total score.

At the end of the chapter you will be able to rate yourself on a report card on the various functions that constitute the intellectual problem-solving capacity.

Now take the tests. Good luck!

Patterns

In this test you have to decide which design **(A, B, C, or D)** fits in the blank area. You have to make a decision within 30 seconds of viewing the figure. Write down your choice and note your time. The higher your score, the greater your ability at abstraction and conceptualization.

FIGURE 1

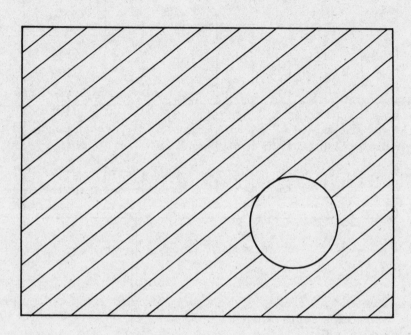

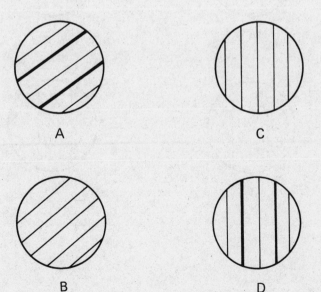

FIGURE 2

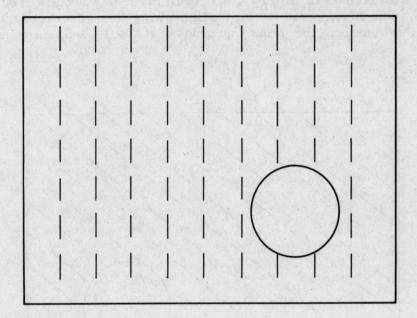

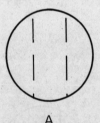

A

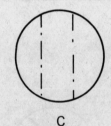

C

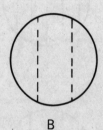

B

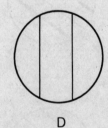

D

FIGURE 3

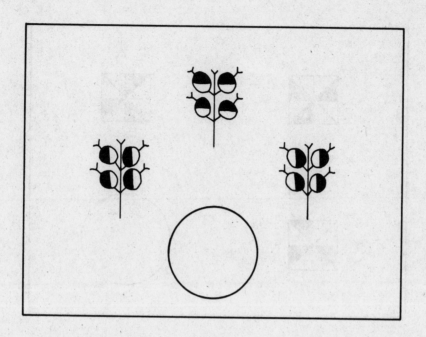

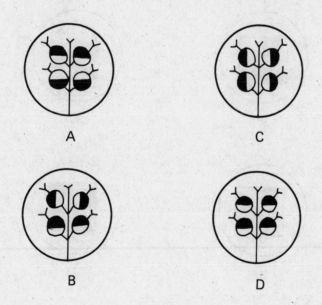

A

C

B

D

FIGURE 4

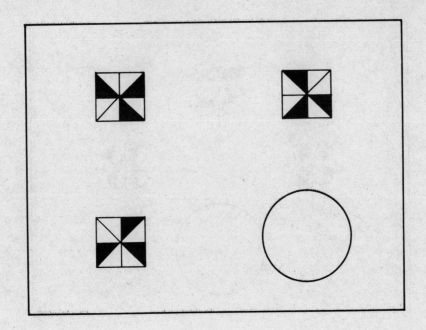

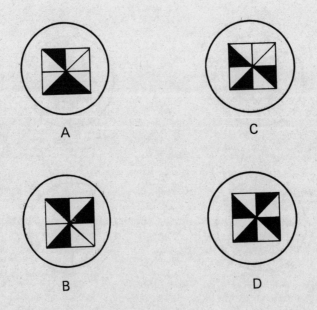

FIGURE 5

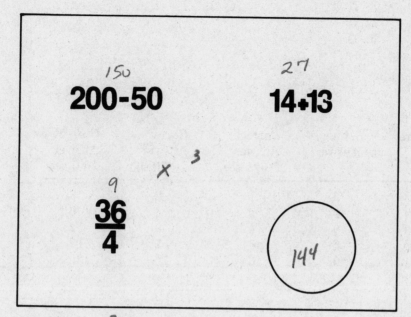

150
200-50

27
14+13

9
36
4

× ³

144

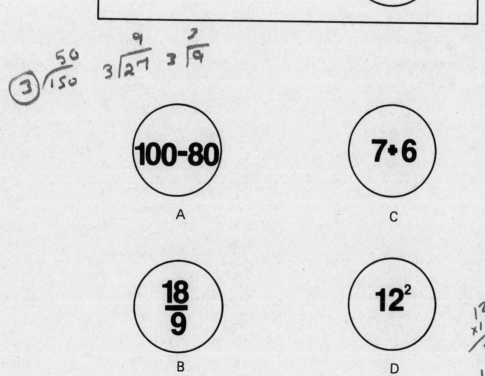

$3\overline{)150}$ = 50 $3\overline{)27}$ = 9 $3\overline{)9}$ = 3

100-80

A

7+6

C

18
9

B

12²

D

12
×12
24
12
144

Answers: Figure 1 B
               2 A
               3 D
               4 B
               5 D

Scoring:

Figure	Wrong Answer	Correct Answer 30-20 sec.	Correct Answer 20-10 sec.	Correct Answer 10-0 sec.
1	0	1	2	3
2	0	2	4	6
3	0	4	8	12
4	0	6	12	18
5	0	10	15	20

Score: Over   23, excellent
         Over   10, very good
         Below 10, fair

20

Blocks

In this test you have to determine the *maximum* number of cubes that could be arranged in the design without being seen (including completely hidden cubes). In order to score you have to write down your answer within 30 seconds after viewing each figure. Time yourself, writing down number of seconds. The greater your score, the greater your ability to conceptualize spatial relationships.

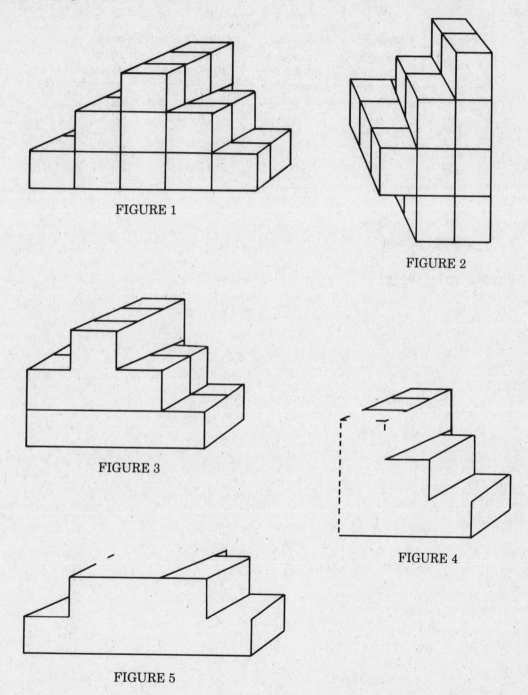

FIGURE 1

FIGURE 2

FIGURE 3

FIGURE 4

FIGURE 5

Answers: Figure   1   24
                     2   22
                     3   21
                     4   15
                     5   21

Scoring:

Figure	Wrong Answer	Correct Answer 30-20 sec.	Correct Answer 20-10 sec.	Correct Answer 10-0 sec.
1	0	2	4	6
2	0	4	6	8
3	0	6	8	10
4	0	8	10	12
5	0	10	15	20

Score: 30-56   Excellent
            20-29   Good
            12-19   Fair
        Below 12   Poor

Incomplete Figures

In this test you have to guess what object or word is hidden in each figure. In order to score you have to write down your answer within 30 seconds after viewing each figure.

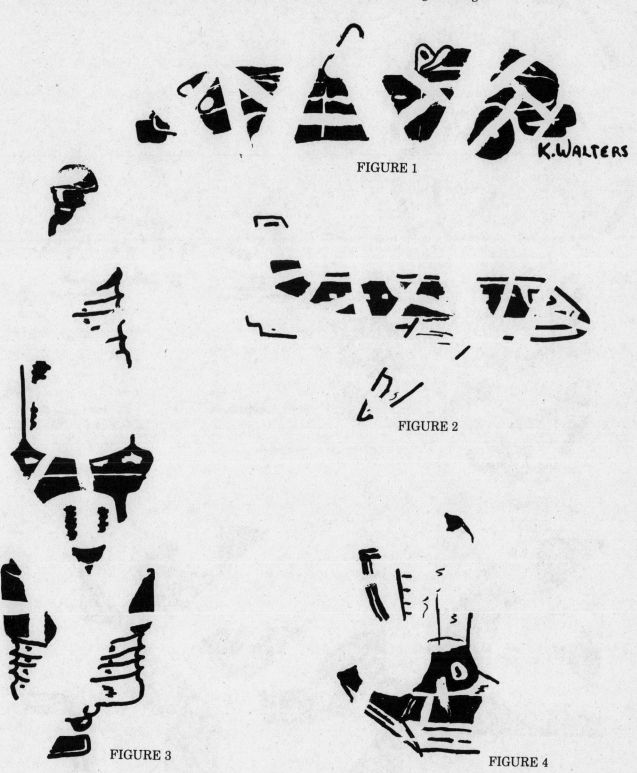

FIGURE 1

FIGURE 2

FIGURE 3

FIGURE 4

FIGURE 5

FIGURE 7

K. WALTERS

FIGURE 6

24

FIGURE 8

FIGURE 9

FIGURE 10

K.WALTERS

Answers: Figure 1 Car
          2 Airplane
          3 Spark plug
          4 Blender
          5 Chandelier
          6 Don't
          7 Toaster
          8 Shirt
          9 Access
         10 Key

Scoring:

Figure	Wrong Answer	Correct Answer 30-20 sec.	Correct Answer 20-10 sec.	Correct Answer 10-0 sec.
1	0	1	2	3
2	0	1	2	3
3	0	2	3	4
4	0	2	3	4
5	0	3	4	5
6	0	3	4	5
7	0	4	5	6
8	0	4	5	6
9	0	5	6	8
10	0	5	6	8

Score: 30-52   Very observant, alert, and able to synthesize from small bits of information

          14-29   Good ability

Below 14   You need complete information before coping

Memory of Figures

This test will check your memory for what you observe. Look at each figure for only 10 seconds. Then cover the figure and draw the same figure from memory within the blank. Try to be as accurate as possible. Do not spend more than 5 minutes on each replication.

FIGURE 1

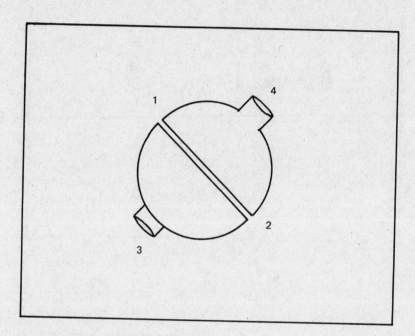

FIGURE 2

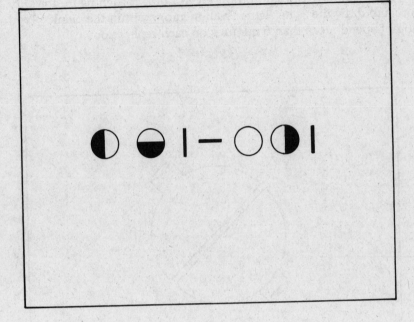

FIGURE 3

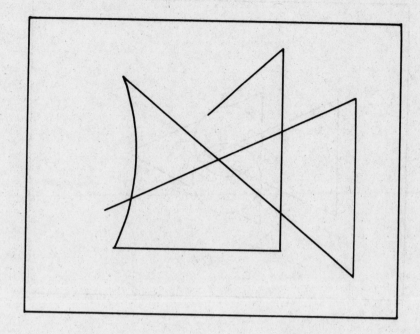

FIGURE 4

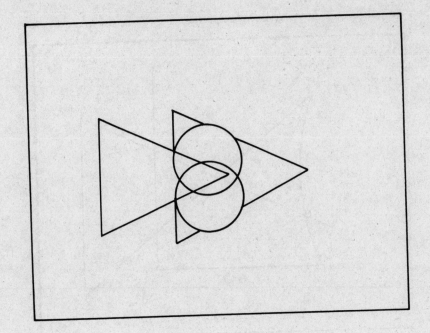

FIGURE 5

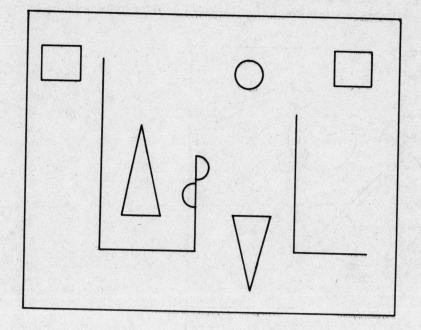

Scoring: Each area in the drawing indicated by a circle in the answer key shows points correct. For total points refer to table below.

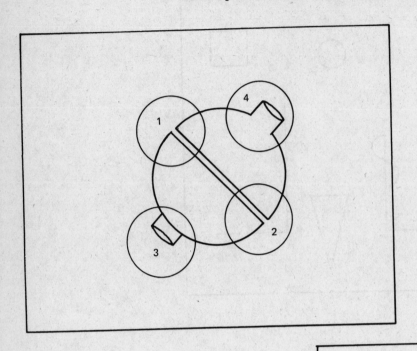

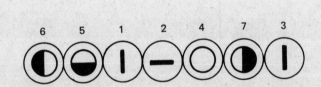

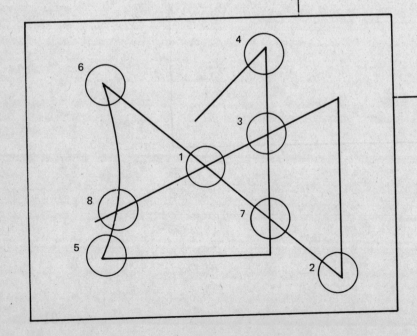

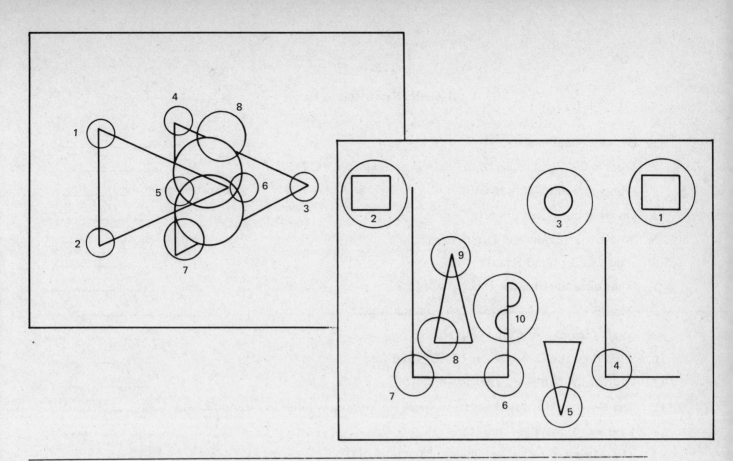

Fig.	Area	Points for Correct Answer	Remarks	Fig.	Area	Points	Fig.	Area	Points	Remarks
1	1	2		3	4	2	5	1	1	Subtract 1
	2	2			5	3		2	1	point for each
	3	3			6	3		3	1	component
	4	4			7	3		4	2	that has been
2	1	1	Subtract 1		8	3		5	2	misplaced
	2	1	point for each	4	1	1		6	2	
	3	1	component in		2	1		7	2	
	4	2	wrong place		3	1		8	2	
	5	3			4	1		9	3	
	6	3			5	3		10	5	
	7	3			6	3				
3	1	1			7	4				
	2	2			8	4				
	3	2								

Score: 60-83   You have a rare ability to perceive and remember forms.
40-59   Very good visual memory.
20-39   Perhaps you can recall sounds well?
Below 20   Very poor memory. Or perhaps very poor vision?

General Knowledge Test

1. Where is Guatemala? _____

2. What is the significance of the date December 7, 1941? _____

3. Who was John Wilkes Booth? _____

4. On what continent is Korea? _____

5. Who wrote **Crime and Punishment**? _____

6. Who was Sigmund Freud? _____

7. What does the formula NaCl stand for? _____

8. What is the average weight of the human brain? _____

9. What is the closest planet to the sun? _____

10. What does the abbreviation OPEC stand for? _____

11. Who wrote **Gulliver's Travels**? _____

12. The Greek orator who learned to speak by keeping pebbles in his mouth was _____

13. Who was Mohandas Gandhi? _____

14. The Alaskan pipeline terminates at the port of _____

15. The confluence of the Blue and White Nile occurs near the city of _____

16. A temperature of 10° Celsius is what in Fahrenheit? _____

17. If it is 4 A.M. in London, what time is it in Chicago? _____

18. Who wrote **The Waste Land**? _____

19. What is a planarian? _____

20. Where is Tasmania? _____

21. What is an abacus? _____

22. Which of the following is toxic to man even in small dosages: Zn, Ca, Pb, Mn, K, or Na? _____

23. What is a sarcophagus? _____

24. Who is the author of **Billy Budd, Foretopman**? _____

25. What does the Greek letter σ stand for statistically? _____

Answers:

1. Central America
2. Bombing of Pearl Harbor by the Japanese
3. Alleged assassin of Abraham Lincoln
4. Asia
5. Dostoyevsky
6. Father of psychoanalysis
7. Salt
8. 3¼ - 3¾ pounds
9. Mercury
10. Organization of Petroleum Exporting Countries
11. Jonathan Swift
12. Demosthenes
13. Great Indian leader, called the Mahatma
14. Valdez
15. Khartoum
16. 50°
17. 10 P.M.
18. T. S. Eliot
19. A flatworm
20. Island South of Australia
21. A simple calculating device
22. Pb
23. A stone coffin
24. Herman Melville
25. Standard deviation

Scoring: Score 1 point for each correct answer.

Score: 20-25   Exceptional knowledge
          15-20   Very good
          10-15   Well read
           5-10   Fair
Below 5   Not well read

Incidental Learning

In this test you'll find out how much you have learned while doing the earlier tests, without having received instructions to remember any particular information. Score your answers at the end of this test. Don't guess; you will be penalized.

Patterns Test

1. How many designs were presented in the patterns test?
   (a) 7   (b) 3   (c) 5   (d) 4

2. How many blank areas were placed at the bottom-right corner of the designs?
   (a) 5   (b) 3   (c) 2   (d) 4

3. How many designs offered five different solutions to choose from?
   (a) 2   (b) 1   (c) 0   (d) 3

4. What was the shape of the pattern?
   (a) square   (b) rectangular   (c) circle   (d) triangular

Blocks Test

5. How many designs were presented?
   (a) 5   (b) 4   (c) 6   (d) 7

6. Which geometrical form was used in the test most often?
   (a) triangle   (b) cube   (c) circle   (d) rectangle

7. In how many designs was the base shorter than the height?
   (a) 3   (b) 2   (c) 1   (d) 0

8. How many blocks did the highest block-column have?
   (a) 3   (b) 4   (c) 5   (d) 6

Incomplete Figures Test

9. Which figure did not appear in the test?
   (a) chandelier   (b) toaster   (c) bicycle   (d) car

10. What kind of airplane appeared in the test?
    (a) jet plane   (b) sail plane   (c) propeller plane

11. Which of the following words appeared in the test?
    (a) expelled   (b) excess   (c) accepted   (d) access   (e) down

12. What automobile part was depicted in one of the pictures?
    (a) wheel   (b) headlight   (c) spark plug   (d) carburetor   (e) cigarette lighter

13. How many designs were presented?
    (a) 4   (b) 3   (c) 6   (d) 5

14. Which geometrical shape was not present in the test?
    (a) trapezoid   (b) hexagon   (c) octagon   (d) all of the above   (e) none of the above

Answers:

1. (c)	8. (b)
2. (d)	9. (c)
3. (c)	10. (c)
4. (b)	11. (d)
5. (a)	12. (c)
6. (b)	13. (d)
7. (c)	14. (d)

Scoring: Score 1 point for each correct answer, subtract 1 point for each incorrect answer, subtract ½ point for each unanswered question.

Score: 6-14   You are highly cognizant of things around you and probably learn very quickly.

         -3-+5   You generally must attend closely to a topic to learn it.

Below -3   You are overconfident in your abilities.

Visual Attention

In this test your visual attention will be examined. In the first part of the test you are to cross out all the 2's and 7's that appear in the six lines. Work fast. You have a maximum of 30 seconds and you are to go over the lines *only once*. In the second part, repeat the same procedure crossing out all the S's and E's. You have another 30 seconds.

1	3	1	8	6	2	X	S	V	C	N	L
3	7	3	7	3	8	G	C	E	Y	V	I
8	1	7	2	2	0	R	E	E	P	L	H
7	0	2	4	1	4	K	L	H	V	S	S
8	9	2	1	6	0	E	W	E	R	C	E
6	5	0	6	5	6	S	W	Q	R	C	D
2	8	5	5	8	2	V	D	D	K	L	D
4	3	8	8	3	4	C	E	L	E	L	C
7	2	3	2	6	7	H	B	L	H	L	L
9	7	2	3	5	7	L	N	S	S	I	L
2	3	7	7	4	9	S	C	Z	T	Z	Y
3	2	5	4	7	5	D	S	A	N	Q	J
7	5	1	5	8	4	E	D	I	P	S	S
6	4	2	2	2	6	J	T	E	S	S	F
2	8	0	7	1	2	Y	I	E	L	S	S
4	8	3	1	6	1	G	L	B	L	V	B
3	5	7	0	4	7	E	K	H	S	N	V
7	7	7	7	0	9	M	J	N	A	E	F
5	2	9	3	2	6	E	S	E	J	F	F
0	4	4	7	3		B	V	G	X	T	F
9	2	7	4	4	4	F	W	E	E	H	H
8	3	2	5	2	7	G	S	K	R	T	H
5	6	1	1	9	2	E	N	I	C	R	
7	5	5	2	3	9	R	F	H	T	G	W
2	9	1	7	7	4	J	E	R	N	S	
6	7	2	6	4	7	S	U	M	F	D	W
3	3	3	4	6	5	T	K	K	R	H	I
5	4	6	0	6	0	F	R	M	O	H	Y

Scoring: Score 1 point for each 2, 7, S, and E crossed out. Subtract 1 point for each 2, 7, S, E, left unmarked and for each incorrect digit or letter crossed out.

Score:
70 - 100	You scan well, work fast, stick to a task, and are highly motivated.
40 - 69	A very good performance; you have motivation.
20 - 39	Your motivation, speed, or perception is in question.
Below 20	You found the test boring and stupid, and saw no sense doing more than one line. Or you may have a perceptual handicap.

What Is Your Trivia Quotient?

1. Where did the dirigible *Hindenberg* crash? _____

2. The 500,000 dogs of New York City contribute how many gallons of urine to city streets each day? _____

3. What was the address of the residence of Fibber McGee and Molly? _____

4. What was the name of Richard Nixon's dog while he was Vice-President? _____

5. How many miles of blood vessels are there in the human body? _____

6. What baseball position did Chuck Connors play? _____

7. Who was Elizabeth Taylor's first husband? _____

8. Who said "We shall have peace in our time"? _____

9. Name the Dionne quintuplets. _____

10. What was the The Shadow's real name? _____

11. Mickey Mouse was to Walt Disney what Woody Woodpecker was to _____

12. On the TV show *I Love Lucy* the Ricardos' close neighbors and friends were the _____

13. What was the gift Sherman Adams received that created a scandal in the Eisenhower Administration? _____

14. Eddie Anderson played what part on the Jack Benny radio program? _____

15. What special apparatus did Howard Hughes design for the movie *The Outlaw?* _____

Answers:

1.	Lakehurst, New Jersey	9.	Annette, Emélie, Yvonne, Cécile, Marie
2.	90,000 gallons	10.	Lamont Cranston
3.	79 Wistfull Vista	11.	Walter Lantz
4.	Checkers	12.	Mertzes
5.	60,000 miles	13.	Vicuna coat
6.	First base	14.	Rochester
7.	Nicky Hilton	15.	Jane Russell's bra
8.	Neville Chamberlain		

Scoring: Score 1 point for each correct answer.

Score:
10 - 15	Master of useless detail
5 - 10	Moderately alert
Below 5	Do not enter any trivia contests

Interpretation of Report Card Scores

Patterns and Blocks

A good problem solver must not only know facts but also must see the relationship between them. People who score high on these two tests are excellent in this ability.

Incomplete Figures

Those who score low here "cannot see the forest for the trees." They get bogged down in detail and frequently miss the main point of an issue.

Memory of Figures

People who score high here are strong in visual creativity. Low scorers on this test probably need a road map to find the lavatory.

General Knowledge Test

This test measures breadth of education.

Incidental Learning and Visual Attention Tests

Both these tests measure your ability to grasp information as facts are thrown at you in rapid-fire fashion.

Test Results

Consider the test scores for Frank Baker, an executive with a large advertising firm (see next page). By examining the pattern of Frank's results you can see that he had an outstanding score on the General Knowledge Test, consistent with his love of reading and high level of education, but showed weakness on the Incidental Learning and Visual Attention tests. Frank was the type of person who hated meetings and lectures with a passion. He would get bored, never learn too much from this type of presentation — even during his college days — and, instead, would take work home from the office to digest it more slowly and at his own pace. The test results confirm why this learning pattern was more effective for him. Frank's attention span and ability to resist distractions were quite poor, as revealed by these two low test scores. He could absorb information best when it was presented in small chunks in a quiet setting, free from extraneous stimuli. His Patterns and Blocks tests revealed that he had an adequate ability to see the interrelationships between issues. His scores on the Incomplete Figures and Memory of Figures tests, respectively, revealed that he was capable of solving problems dealing with symbolic logic (such as drawing conclusions from the jumble of figures in an annual report) and could evoke imaginative solutions to complex issues.

Now fill in your test scores on the blank report card and assess your problem-solving abilities.

Report Card for Problem Solving

Frank Baker, Account Executive

Tests	Low		Medium		High	
Patterns	0	10	11	22	23	59
Blocks	0	12	13	25	26	56
Incomplete Figures	0	14	15	29	30	52
Memory of Figures	0	17	18	45	46	83
General Knowledge Test	0	10	11	17	18	25
Incidental Learning	0	3	4	8	9	14
Visual Attention	0	25	26	49	50	100

Instructions: Go back to each of the tests included in this report card and transfer your score by placing an X on the score you obtained. Your overall standing will be indicated by where the majority of the X symbols are placed.

Report Card for Problem Solving

Tests	Low		Medium		High	
Patterns	0	10	11 ✖	22	23	59
Blocks	0	12	13 ✖	25	26	56
Incomplete Figures	0	14	15 ✖	29	30	52
Memory of Figures	0	17	18 ✖	45	46	83
General Knowledge Test	0	10	11	17	18 ✖	25
Incidental Learning	0 ✖	3	4	8	9	14
Visual Attention	0 ✖	25	26	49	50	100

2 Where's Your Common Sense?

I am sure you must know someone who never completed college and maybe even dropped out of high school but who, nevertheless, is an enormous success in life. Or, you might know someone to whom many people intuitively turn for advice even though that person is not a professional counselor. Somehow, certain individuals are able to distill great amounts of wisdom out of their life experience. These people are said to possess much common sense — a capacity that may be correlated but is not necessarily synonymous with intellectual problem-solving abilities.

In this chapter you will take several tests that will rate your capacities to make judgments based on practical wisdom or "common sense." None of the answers to these questions requires higher education or a broad fund of knowledge. What is being measured here is your ability to see through the complexities of situations and come up with practical solutions that will help you get along well in life.

A. As James was looking out his window that morning, nothing of particular interest seemed to draw his attention. Glendale Street in the London Borough of Westminster seemed to be still asleep. Being a government employee, he was expected to appear in his office on time. Today he was scheduled to report his findings to his boss, head of Military Intelligence. Two matters were bothering James. Though only his superior knew about his assignment, he had a nagging feeling that Jackson, the supervisor of Internal Affairs in their department, who occupied an office across the hall, always seemed to be in the corridor when James went to see General Moore. The other troubling fact was that Jackson had recently moved into an apartment in the same building James lived in. Jackson explained his move by showing James his new white Mercedes: "A private driveway and garage in this building and at that price is quite a find these days."

James knew now much more about what he was assigned to find out, and knew that it would be wise to take some precautions on his way to the office. He couldn't brush aside the feeling that someone had been following him in the street. Since the door of his apartment let into the street to the right of Jackson's driveway, he would make sure nothing surprising was coming out of there, and crossing to the other side of the street, would catch a cab going downtown. Halfway downtown, James thought, it would be a good idea to change cabs and head uptown, where his office really was. James was somewhat nervous as he opened his front door. There was little traffic in the street. Hurriedly he locked the door, glanced to the left toward the driveway and the street, and not seeing any car, he began crossing the street. He managed to take two steps . . . before all turned dark after being hit by the front bumper of a car. He thought to himself, "Damn it! Where did that car appear from? There was no car in the street its entire length!" Then he lost consciousness. To the experienced policeman it seemed that the driver of the blue Mercedes was telling the truth, saying he didn't mean to hit the man who just stepped into the street not looking where he was going. Jackson appeared at the office that day somewhat late.

The question is: Why didn't James see the approaching (or waiting) car?

B. A marksman, in an attempt to demonstrate his skill, hammered a nail into a tree, hung up his new hat, placed his rifle on his shoulder pointing back, walked fifty feet from the tree, and while his back was to the tree he fired. Upon examination of the hat, it was clearly demonstrated by the fresh bullet hole that the marksman had hit his target.

The question is: How did he hit his hat without taking visual aim (no mirrors were used)?

Answers:

A. James didn't see the approaching car because he looked the wrong way. To what degree did you get trapped by the elaborate build-up and fail to see the obvious?

B. He hung his hat on the end of his rifle. Again, did the obvious elude you? Are you prone to overly complicate things or can you cut through the forest quickly and see the trees?

These two tests are illustrative of that capacity we know as common sense. The following tests will help you assess factors in your approach to problems that will help you see how gifted or deficient you are in this capacity.

Operating in Traffic

This test will tell you how aware you are of hazardous situations involving vehicles and pedestrians. Inspect each figure carefully before answering the questions.

FIGURE 1

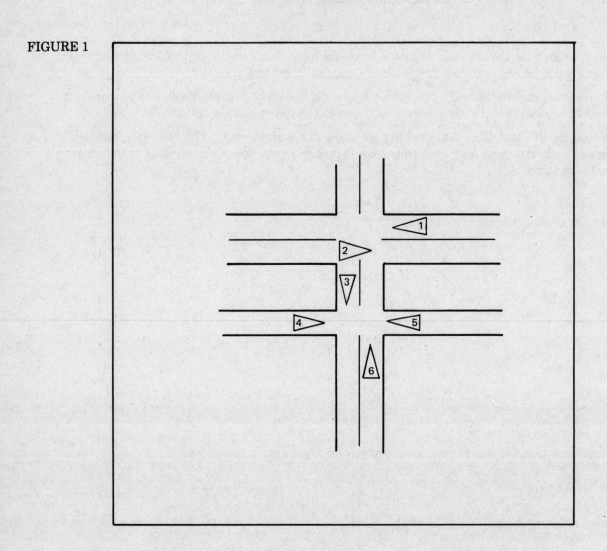

Figure 1: Which car (s) ought to give the right of way to which car (s)?

    (a)   1 to 2
    (b)   3 to 5
    (c)   4 to 3
    (d)   6 to 5
    (e)   4 to 6
    (f)   both (b) and (e)
    (g)   both (a) and (d)
    (h)   both (d) and (e)

FIGURE 2

Figure 2: Which car (s) ought to give the right of way to which car (s)?

     (a)   1 to 2
     (b)   3 to 4
     (c)   5 to 7
     (d)   7 to 5
     (e)   6 to 2
     (f)   8 to 9
     (g)   9 to 8
     (h)   8 to 5
     (i)   both (b) and (c)
     (j)   both (d) and (f)
     (k)   both (e) and (d)

FIGURE 3   FIGURE 4

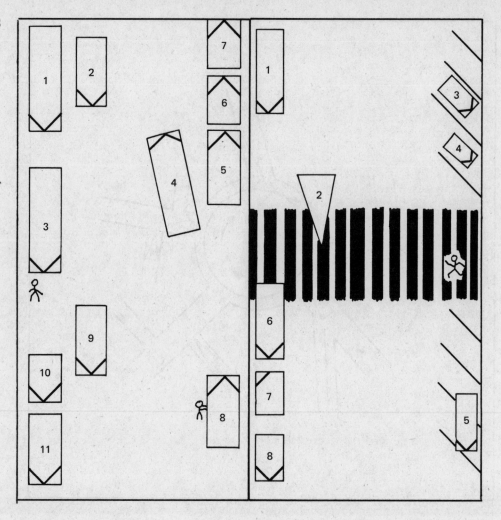

Figure 3:   Truck 4 is parallel parking between car 5 and car 8. What is a violation in the figure? (One answer only)

Figure 4:   Who could be ticketed by a policeman in this situation?

Answers:

Figure 1   (h)

Figure 2   (j)

Figure 3   There should be an assistant to guide the truck driver from the rear while backing up the truck.

Figure 4   Car 2, Car 5, and Car 6.

Scoring: Score 1 point for each correct answer in Figures 1 through 3; in Figure 4, score 1 point for each detected violation.

Are You Rational?

Check either True or False.   True   False

1. You read your horoscope more than once a week.

2. You pray daily.

3. You are careful to avoid walking under ladders.

4. Before you married your spouse or before you get involved
    with someone, you are eager to know your partner's sign.

5. UFOs are from outer space.

6. You believe in reincarnation.

7. You know someone who has ESP.

8. You contacted a spirit at a séance.

Scoring: Score 1 point for each "False" you checked. This test measures the degree to which
you rely on rational means in evaluating events and experiences. Being superational is often
associated with a lack of humanity.

Score: 5-8   Superrational
          1-5   Like most of us
          0   Heavy on beliefs, light on facts

How Impressionable Are You?

The following test will indicate how impressionable a person you are. Answer the questions by circling the appropriate degree.

		Never				Always
1.	When dressing, I take the weather forecast into account.	1	2	3	4	5
2.	When I don't feel like smoking but someone offers me a cigarette, I accept it.	1	2	3	4	5
3.	When I don't feel well, and someone says I look bad, I feel worse.	1	2	3	4	5
4.	When my partner wants to go to a movie and I don't, I change my mind.	1	2	3	4	5
5.	When at a party I don't feel like drinking but someone offers me a drink, I accept it.	1	2	3	4	5
6.	When someone says he/she likes my haircut, I try to have an identical haircut next time.	1	2	3	4	5
7.	When someone tells me I should lose weight, I think of it when I eat my next meal.	1	2	3	4	5
8.	If a friend really tried, he/she would succeed in getting me to gamble.	1	2	3	4	5
9.	I can be persuaded to have sex even when I don't feel like it.	1	2	3	4	5
10.	Even when I am really not hungry, I can be persuaded to eat.	1	2	3	4	5

Scoring: Tally the numbers you circled. If you scored between 10 and 20 points, you are quite unsusceptible to the influence of others. If you scored between 40 and 50 points, you are overly impressionable and ought perhaps to learn to make your own decisions, believe in them, and more important, stick to them. The 20 to 40 point range is the average degree of suggestibility in people.

Common Sense Inventory

This test will tell you how much common sense you use in your everyday life. Simply answer each question by checking either Yes or No.

Yes   No

1. Have you drawn up a will?

2. Do you have a list of your credit card numbers?

3. Do you regularly check the tire pressure and tread depth on your car?

4. Do you have an insurance policy with a cost-of-living clause?

5. Do you get a physical examination at least once every two years?

6. Have you given up or do you avoid smoking?

7. Do you have extra keys for your home and car?

8. Do you keep a written record of your expenses and the receipts?

9. Do you regularly check the weather forecast before you go out for the day?

10. Do you keep the telephone numbers of the fire and police departments in a prominent place?

Scoring: Score 1 point for each Yes answer.

Score: 0-3   You should marry someone who could take care of you.

               4-6   Average

               7-10   High level of common sense

Interpretation of Report Card Scores

Operating in Traffic

Complex problems often require simple solutions. Nowhere is a deficiency in common sense more obvious than in the way some people drive their cars. A high score on this test is indicative of solid common sense.

Are You Rational?

The more skeptical you are about unprovable phenomena, such as horoscopes and UFOs (Captain Kirk, forgive me), the more common sense you possess. This test measures your need for rational rather than mystical or superstitious explanations for everyday phenomena.

How Impressionable Are You?

The less you are swayed by the opinions of others, the more likely it is that you possess good common sense. This test shows to what extent you subscribe to the maxim "I'm from Missouri — show me."

Common Sense Inventory

This test assesses just how much of a role common sense plays in your everyday life.

Report Card for Common Sense

Tests	Low		Medium		High	
Operating in Traffic	0	2	3	4	5	7
Are You Rational?	0	2	3	5	6	10
How Impressionable Are You?	50	41	40	21	20	10
Common Sense Inventory	0	3	4	6	7	10

Instructions: Go back to each of the tests included in this report card and transfer your score by placing an X on the score you obtained. Your overall standing will be indicated by where the majority of the X symbols are placed.

3 How Creative Are You?

All of us envy creative people especially those who have gained the limelight such as movie directors, scientists, the developer of a new product that takes off in sales, and just plain people who seem to find short-cut solutions to difficult problems. It is a fact that most people are unaware of how truly creative they are. Fear of humiliation and ridicule more often robs people of creativity than lack of endowment. It takes guts to strike out on your own and create something novel. It requires even more determination and courage to subject your creative efforts to the opinions of others.

These tests will help you assess your creative potential. After their completion, you will have some idea of how the world is likely to respond to your creative endeavors.

Verbal Creativity 1

This test will tell you how creative you are under time and visual pressure. You have to hold the following crossword puzzle as printed (upside down), and within *three* minutes write down as many words as you can recognize. Time yourself accurately.

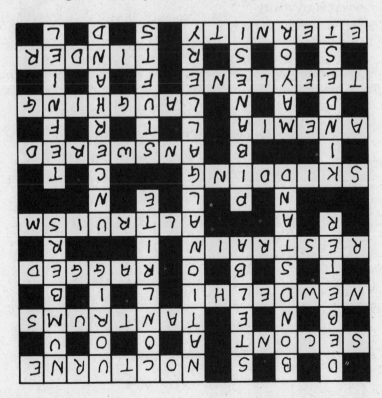

Answers:

> nocturne, tantrums, New Delhi, ragged, restrain, altruism, skidding, answered, anemia, laughing, tinder, eternity, National Gallery, numbers, kindest, mayor

Scoring: For each recognized word (within 3 minutes) score 1 point.

Score: 0-4   Poor verbal creativity
5-8   Fair verbal creativity
9-12   Good verbal creativity
13-16   Excellent verbal creativity

Verbal Creativity 2

This test is designed to establish how good you are at creating words under time pressure. You will have three minutes to form as many words as you can from the word given below. (Example: from the word elevator you can form the words or, at, vale, tale, rote, etc.) The words you have formed must have a meaning (appearing in the dictionary).

The word is: CONFRONTATION

Scoring: Score 1 point for each word you formed.

Score:

	0-5	Poor verbal creativity
	5-10	Fair verbal creativity
	10-20	Good verbal creativity
More than	20	Very good verbal creativity

In case you're wondering, below are some of the words you could have extracted from the word CONFRONTATION. There are considerably more than 20 here — and perhaps even more.

1)	CON	14)	ION	27)	FOR
2)	FIRN	15)	CAN'T	28)	FIT
3)	TON	16)	ROT	29)	FRONT
4)	TIN	17)	COT	30)	TORN
5)	NOT	18)	RAT	31)	CANNOT
6)	TAN	19)	FIR	32)	THAT
7)	TRAIN	20)	TOT	33)	NOR
8)	RAIN	21)	TROT	34)	ROOF
9)	NOTION	22)	FAT	35)	CAN
10)	NATION	23)	IRON	36)	FAN
11)	NOTATION	24)	CAR	37)	RATION
12)	NOON	25)	FIN		
13)	ROTATION	26)	FAR		

Functional Fixedness Test

Some people can think of only one use for certain objects (example: pencil — to write with) and cannot conceive of any other helpful use (example: to make holes in a piece of cloth or paper when the need arises). This inability is called functional fixedness. Are you such a "functional fixed" person? This test will tell you. In this test you have to be your own judge. For each item try to generate three different uses which you deem to be legitimate possibilities.

1. Postage stamp
   1. _____
   2. _____
   3. _____

2. Pliers
   1. _____
   2. _____
   3. _____

3. Candle
   1. _____
   2. _____
   3. _____

4. Chewing gum
   1. _____
   2. _____
   3. _____

5. Chair
   1. _____
   2. _____
   3. _____

6. Bottle caps
   1. _____
   2. _____
   3. _____

7. Bed sheet
   1. _____
   2. _____
   3. _____

8. Chalk
   1. _____
   2. _____
   3. _____

Scoring: For each "logical" use you could think of, score 1 point.

Score: 8-13   High degree of functional fixedness

14-17   Middle-range functional fixedness

18-24   Low functional fixedness; high level of creativity and possibly good problem-solving skills

Concept Formation Test

This test will examine your skills at categorizing. In each of the following items you will find several words that belong to one category or concept whereas the others do not. (Example: candle, match, competition, lighter, fire, flint. The category is ignition tools. Correct words: match, lighter, flint.) Always form the concept which has the largest number of words.

1. Car, wheel, bicycle, doughnut, elevator, ring, stairway, helm
2. Chair, pillow, bed, couch, rug, floor, window, paint
3. Table, fork, knife, cloth, cabinet, saw, tree, ax, food, scissors
4. Hose, glass, ditch, bucket, aquaduct, pot, pitcher
5. Green, black, red, brown, paint, yellow, white, color, blue
6. Pants, shirt, gloves, socks, vest, shoes, mittens, sweater
7. Dog, cat, snake, rabbit, shark, man, whale, monkey, jaws
8. Inch, meter, kilo, yard, once, stone, foot, volt, watt
9. Bay, river, peninsula, lagoon, fjord, island, lake, fountain
10. Fight, white, far, sea, fat, low, fagot, roach, flint, fire

Answers:

1. Wheel, doughnut, ring, helm -- objects with holes
2. Chair, bed, couch — furniture
3. Knife, saw, ax, scissors — tools to cut with
4. Glass, bucket, pot, pitcher — containers
5. Green, red, yellow, blue — colors of the spectrum
6. Gloves, socks, shoes, mittens — worn on one's extremities
7. Dog, cat, rabbit, man, whale, monkey — mammals
8. Inch, meter, yard, foot — measures of distance
9. Bay, river, lagoon, fjord — bodies of water connected to the sea
10. Fight, fat, fagot, flint — words which start with "F" and end with "T"

Scoring: For each completely correct answer score 8 points. For partial answers, score 1 point for each word included only if you had *at least three words* in the item.

Score: 0-20 Poor concept-formation skill
        21-60 Average
        61-80 Very good

Interpretation of Report Card Scores

Verbal Creativity 1 and 2	People who do well on these tests are very fluent, probably exceptional readers, whizzes at Scrabble, and should do well with any problem involving abstract ideas.
Functional Fixedness Test	This test is a measure of your resourcefulness. The more variations you can make on a theme, the more creative you are.
Concept Formation Test	This extremely important test measures your ability to assess and sort through a mass of data and pick out the essential items. The mark of the creative mind is its ability to simplify without being simplistic. A high score on this test should encourage you to try out your creativity on the world.

Test Results

"Tell me, how creative is it to change diapers and run the washing machine twice a day?" Bernice asked me. "I've got a degree with a major in English literature and the maximum use it gets is writing notes to the milkman," she said in some anguish. After we got to discussing her life some more, it was clear that Bernice's choosing the role of housewife and mother was a cop-out. She had always been afraid of failure, and so when the choice came — career or marriage — she hid her talents behind the latter. The pain and frustration she suffered got too hard to bear after her second child was born and she became depressed.

Bernice's case is not too dissimilar from those of many people I see in my psychiatric practice — people who know they are creative but are afraid to rely on their talents as a career base. If you want to know just how much untapped potential Bernice was hiding behind her kitchen counter, just examine her test results below. After she realized that she had what it took, Bernice decided to resume her career aspirations as a writer. Her first manuscript has just been sent to a publisher. I know she will do well.

Now, fill in your own report card and see just how much creative talent you have been hiding all these years.

Report Card for Creativity

Bernice Everson, Housewife and Mother

Tests	Low		Medium		High	
Verbal Creativity 1	0	5	6	10	11 ✱	16
Verbal Creativity 2	0	7	8	14	15 ✱	21+
Functional Fixedness	8	13	14	17	18 ✱	24
Concept Formation	0	20	21	60	61 ✱	80

Instructions: Go back to each of the tests included in this report card and transfer your score by placing an X on the score you obtained. Your overall standing will be indicated by where the majority of the X symbols are placed.

Report Card for Creativity

Tests	Low		Medium		High	
Verbal Creativity 1	0	5	6	10	11	16
Verbal Creativity 2	0	7	8	14	15	21+
Functional Fixedness	8	13	14	17	18	24
Concept Formation	0	20	21	60	61	80

4 How Fast Are Your Reflexes?

Do your ski tips always get crossed? Do you frequently ask yourself, "Who put a hole in my tennis racket?" Are you convinced that some diabolically malicious person made typewriter keys and calculator push-buttons too close together just to confound and frustrate you? Some of us have great difficulty mastering skills requiring dexterity and coordination. Yet many of these skills are necessary for the performance of vocational tasks and recreational activities. If your work or hobby relies a great deal on dexterity and coordination, then you should know just how skilled you are in these capacities.

The tests in this chapter measure some important dexterity and coordination functions. After taking the tests you will be able to rate your overall capacities by filling in your results on the report card at the end of the chapter. Try to combine speed and dexterity to get the best scores you possibly can.

Visual Memory and Motor Coordination

This test will tell you something about your ability to imagine or remember something and your ability to correlate finger movements (fine dexterity) to what you imagine. You will need a watch or clock for this test. Follow the instructions accurately.

Step 1:   Set the clock at 12 o'clock.

Step 2:   Advance the hand to 1 o'clock.

Step 3:   Advance the hand to 3 o'clock.

Step 4:   Advance to 3:30.

Step 5:   Advance to 4 o'clock.

Step 6:   Go back to 2 o'clock.

Step 7:   Go back to 1:30.

Step 8:   Go back to 12 o'clock.

Cover the clock with a piece of cloth so that you cannot see the dial.

Step 9:   Now move the hand to 1 o'clock. Remove the cloth. Look at your setting, mark it down then return the hand to 12 o'clock. Cover with cloth.

Step 10:   Advance to 2:30. Look. Mark. Return to 12 o'clock. Cover.

Step 11:   Set at 3:15. Look. Mark. Return to 12 o'clock. Cover.

Step 12:   Set at 4:45. Look. Mark. Return to 12 o'clock. Cover.

Step 13:   Set at 1:15. Look. Mark. Return to 12 o'clock. Cover.

Step 14:   Set at 11:15. Look. Mark. Return to 12 o'clock. Cover.

Step 15:   Set at 10:45. Look. Mark. Return to 12 o'clock. Cover.

Step 16:   Set at 9 o'clock. Look. Mark. Return to 12 o'clock. Cover.

Step 17:   Set at 10 o'clock. Look. Mark. Return to 12 o'clock. Cover.

Step 18:   Set at 11 o'clock. Look. Mark. Return to 12 o'clock. Cover.

Scoring: For each of Steps 9 through 18 score as follows:

2 points if you set the time within a 5-minute range of the requested time.

1 point if you set the time within a 10-minute range of the requested time.

0 point if your setting was off by more than 10 minutes.

Score: 16-20   Very precise imagery and fine-motor coordination.

        9-15   Above average in upper part of score range, average in lower part of range.

        0-8   Poor to average imagery. You may still have good fine-motor coordination when you receive visual-feedback. Try next test.

Eye-Hand Coordination

This test will assess your fine-motor coordination with and without visual help. For this test you'll need a box of at least 30 wooden matches. On a sheet of white paper draw a square 2½ by 2½ inches. Now follow the instructions accurately.

Step 1: With three matches build a pyramid in the center of the square. You get three tries. Each time you don't succeed, note how many matches fell outside (including partially outside) the square. Score 10 points for success. Subtract 1 point for each match falling outside the square. Maximum score, 10 points; minimum, -9 points.

Step 2: Without taking your eyes off the design given below, try to replicate it within the borders of the square. You have 60 seconds to complete it. Score 25 points for success (all match heads in right direction, all seven matches within the square, ¼-inch protrusions allowed). Subtract 1 point for each error (incorrect direction, or position, over ¼-inch protrusion outside of square). Maximum score, 25 points; minimum, -21 points.

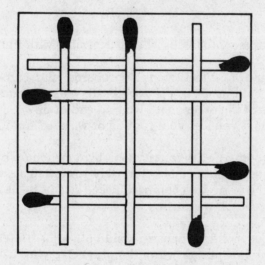

Step 3: Take a matchbox holding 30 wooden matches all pointing in same direction. Empty box on table under a cloth cover. You have 60 seconds to replace matches in box, all pointing in one direction. Score 25 points for success (all in, all in one direction). Subtract 1 point for each match pointing the wrong way. Maximum score, 25 points; minimum, -15 points (providing you replaced all matches).

Scoring: Total your score for all three steps.

Score: -45-0 Your fine-motor coordination needs some practice. Check on which step you did poorest. Check how much visual help you need. Being relaxed plays an important role.

0-30 Not bad at all. With more practice and self-control you should be able to get your fine-motor coordination into the above-average range. Check which step needs improvement most.

31-60 Very good. You must be relaxed and concentrated in addition to possessing good fine-motor coordination. You either are or should be a brain surgeon.

Touch

This test will assess your fingers' sensitivity to familiar objects. You'll need four quarters, four dimes, four nickels, and four pennies. Wear a blindfold or hang a cloth over your face. Shuffle the coins on the table. Now *rapidly*, separate the sum of 80 cents to one side. Did you succeed? Uncover your eyes and check. Return the separated coins to the rest. Repeat same procedure for the following sums: 93 cents; $1.25; $1.33; $1.07; 68 cents; 49 cents; $1.62.

Scoring: Score 1 point for each successful step.

Score: 0-2   Poor finger sensitivity

        3-5   Average finger sensitivity

        6-8   Very good finger sensitivity

Gross-Motor Skills

This test aims to assess your gross-motor skills when performing with full visual feedback.

Step 1: Determine a straight line of 30 feet (along floorboards, tiles, carpet edge, or lay down a clothesline). Holding both hands straight overhead, walk forward on line, the heel of one foot touching the toes of the other foot. Walk to end of line. Score 10 points for complete success. No score if you lost your footing or wavered from line.

Step 2: Stand on one side of room. Focus your gaze on light switch on opposite wall. Stretch one arm forward, index finger pointing. March briskly toward light switch. Touch switch with finger, without wavering or slowing approach pace (do not break finger). Score 10 points for success, no score if switch was missed.

Step 3: Stand upright with your feet 2 feet apart. Hold both arms stretched upward over head, palms facing. With one sweeping downward motion clap your hands behind your back. Score 10 points if your palms met, no score if they did not.

Scoring: Total your score for all three steps.

Score: 0-10   Poor gross-motor coordination

       11-20   Adequate gross-motor coordination

       21-30   Good gross-motor coordination

Do you Know Where You're At?

This test will show you how well you know your body structure. Stand straight, feet together. Close your eyes. Stretch right arm forward (parallel to floor), index finger pointing. Without opening your eyes, in one motion touch with index finger the following body parts, pausing at least 30 seconds between one step and the next. Mark success or failure in appropriate column. Rest two minutes and repeat same procedure with left hand.

| | Right Hand | | | Left Hand | |
	Hit	Miss		Hit	Miss
1. Tip of nose	____	____		____	____
2. Lips	____	____		____	____
3. Center of forehead	____	____		____	____
4. Right knee	____	____		____	____
5. Left elbow (with right hand only)	____	____		____	____
6. Left knee	____	____		____	____
7. Right elbow (with left hand only)	____	____		____	____

Scoring: Tally the "hits" for each hand. If you are right-handed, multiply the *left-hand* score by two. If you are left-handed, multiply the *right-hand* score by two. Now add both scores.

Score: 0-7   Poor body knowledge
       8-14   Average body knowledge
       15-21 Good body knowledge

Are You Really a Lefty or a Righty?

This test aims to determine your true laterality. There are people who are "right-handed" but may also have strong left-handed leanings. Answer the following statements by circling either L (left) or R (right) representing the body part you most often use when engaging in the described activity.

1.	I sign checks with my . . .	L	R	(hand)
2.	I cut steak with my . . .	L	R	(hand)
3.	I peek through a keyhole with my . . .	L	R	(eye)
4.	I kick a ball with my . . .	L	R	(foot)
5.	I hold the phone to my . . .	L	R	(ear)
6.	I pull a bowstring with my . . .	L	R	(hand)
7.	I throw a ball with my . . .	L	R	(hand)
8.	When not hearing clearly, I cup my . . .	L	R	(ear)
9.	I wink with my . . .	L	R	(eye)
10.	I mount a bicycle with my . . .	L	R	(foot)
11.	I ring a doorbell with my . . .	L	R	(hand)
12.	When I ponder, I tilt my head to the . . .	L	R	(side)
13.	I carry my purse or briefcase on my . . .	L	R	(shoulder)
14.	When kneeling on one knee, the one on the ground is the . . .	L	R	(knee)
15.	I scratch my head with my . . .	L	R	(hand)
16.	I pick up change with my . . .	L	R	(hand)

Scoring: If you indicated a preference for your dominant side (i.e., left or right) in no more than twelve or thirteen of the sixteen statements, there is a good chance you are not a true "righty" or "lefty."

Memory and Coordination Test and Eye-Hand Coordination Test	The ability to translate thought into action is a key element in learning. If you did poorly on these tests, you probably should stick to tasks that don't require too much manual dexterity or prolonged mental manipulations. If you are a brain surgeon and scored poorly, make sure you keep up the premiums on your malpractice insurance.
Touch Test	Can you "see" with your fingers as do skilled mechanics, top-rated typists, and (forgive me, but it's true) excellent lovers? A high score on this test should embolden you to take up any one of the above.
Gross-Motor Skills Test / Do You Know Where You're At?	Your scores on these tests should correlate quite well with your tennis and golf performance. Good athletes always score high on these tests.
Lefty or Righty?	You should be able to coordinate all activities performed with all parts of the body. That involves a capacity called dominance. Or, more simply put, being a "righty" or a "lefty." Some people are mixtures of right- and left-dominant, perhaps writing with their left hand, but kicking a soccer ball with their right foot. Severe learning problems can occur in people with mixed dominance (a technical euphemism for "confused dominance"). Your test results here might explain why you found it so difficult to get your reading speed up in college, or why you smashed the typewriter given to you by your uncle as a graduation gift.

Test Results

Bob, despite being careful with money — his and other people's — had spent untold sums trying to become a scratch golfer. "There's a lot of business transacted on the golf course," he rationalized to his wife. In actuality, he was a perfectionist and couldn't tolerate the idea of not being able to master the game. When you examine his test scores below, it will be readily apparent why he will never break par or even approach it. He plods on nevertheless, blaming his golf instructor, or the weather, or his clubs, or the distractions around him for his missed shots. He is simply not coordinated enough to play this game well. A more appropriate exercise for him would be jogging or sex.

Now fill in your report card to see how you rate on dexterity and coordination. Are you in the wrong vocation or pursuing the wrong sport?

Report Card for Dexterity and Coordination

Bob Dawson, Accountant

Tests	Low		Medium		High	
Memory and Coordination	0	8	9 ✗	15	16	20
Eye-Hand Coordination	-45	0	1 ✗	30	31	60
Touch	0 ✗	2	3 ✗	5	6	8
Gross-Motor Skills	0 ✗	10	11	20	21	30
Do You Know Where You're At?	0 ✗	7	8	14	15	21

Instructions: Go back to each of the tests included in this report card and transfer your score by placing an X on the score you obtained. Your overall standing will be indicated by where the majority of the X symbols are placed.

Report Card for Dexterity and Coordination

Tests	Low		Medium		High	
Memory and Coordination	0	8	9	15	16	20
Eye-Hand Coordination	-45	0	1	30	31	60
Touch	0	2	3	5	6	8
Gross-Motor Skills	0	10	11	20	21	30
Do You Know Where You're At?	0	7	8	14	15	21

5 How Moody Are You?

Emotions give life its flavor. Without them, we would go through experiences as did Mr. Spock of *Star Trek* fame; though efficient and logical, he was boring and remote as a companion. Emotions can also complicate our lives, as anyone knows who has tried to solve problems while in a bad mood. In order to better manage your emotional life you should know what your predominant moods are, how widely your feelings tend to fluctuate, how you respond emotionally when your inhibitions are overcome by alcohol, and how you react emotionally to various life circumstances.

The tests in this chapter will help you identify your emotional tendencies under a wide range of situations. Knowing our innermost feelings is a great asset but one we mistakenly don't use when we need it most — that is, when under stress and when we should be taking effective action to cope. Usually we "shoot from the hip" instead, ignoring the emotions we should be trying to understand.

The best way to respond under pressure is to recognize your emotional reactions and *combine them with logic*. In this way you will reach a solution that fits both your emotional needs and the realities of the challenging situation.

When you have analyzed the results of the tests in this chapter, write up a short paragraph describing your emotions. Memorize it. By knowing your emotional profile you will avoid many painful situations and will learn to be effective as well as compassionate.

MOODINESS

"Color Me" Test

This test is designed to tell you something about your emotional tendencies. You are to color the following 5 figures (of your own sex only). Color the figures as you imagine *yourself* in the five described situations (dating, job interview, going to work, at a party, entertaining at home). Use pencils or felt-tip pens in the following colors: yellow, red, blue, green. Use as many of these colors as you want and color every space in the figure's outline.

DATING

Scoring: Each color is believed to represent an emotional tendency. For each situation, using the scoring figures, determine which color of the four was allotted the highest percentage of space. Using the color key that follows, you can fairly well determine in which mood you see yourself, and hence which personality style you project, in each situation.

Hair –	5%
Face –	10%
Neck –	5%
Shirt, Blouse –	6%
Jacket, Sweater, Vest, Accessories (handbag, briefcase, etc.) –	25%
Arm R –	4%
Arm L –	4%
Hand R –	4%
Hand L –	4%
Pants, Skirt –	25%
Shoe R –	4%
Shoe L –	4%

Color Key:

Highest % yellow   You are intrigued, curious about new situations. You learn new things and are able to apply them. You have sophisticated thinking patterns which make you a good problem solver. Your everyday life is active and you gain from many different experiences. You have good ideas for smooth social interaction and you are a worthwhile employee. You may be a bit impulsive.

Highest % red   You plunge into situations head first. You enjoy a challenge, and want to come out on top in any interaction. You are quite warm and happy and are willing to get off readily even in the more intimate interactions. You are helpful to others, particularly when they agree with you. One would be happy to have you on (and at) one's side, if one doesn't mind coming second.

Highest % blue   In most situations you are quite relaxed and accepting of others. You are helpful, but you have to be guided. In some situations you may find yourself offended, perhaps due to your sensitivity. Your ability to understand other people helps you through, but too much indecisiveness on your part limits the help you can render others.

Highest % Green   You are a bit pushy, a characteristic which could help you when you need to stand up for your rights. But you tend to overdo it at times, and this may hurt others. You do not like to feel rebuffed, but your assertiveness prevents you from backing off. You lack sensitivity in social interactions, at work and at home. Be independent all you like, but remember that other people like to eat cake too.

Blue Mood Barometer

Answer the following statements by circling the number which most accurately describes your mood as affected by the situation described.

1. I don't feel sad at all.	2. I feel slightly sad.	3. I feel moderately sad.	4. I feel quite sad.	5. I feel extremely sad.

A.	I just had a fight with my best friend.	1	2	3	4	5
B.	My boss notified me that I'll have to take a cut in salary.	1	2	3	4	5
C.	My mother has just called to tell me she heard bad news from her doctor.	1	2	3	4	5
D.	I think my boy/girl friend (husband/wife) seems interested in another.	1	2	3	4	5
E.	I just discovered that I was short-changed by a department store clerk.	1	2	3	4	5
F.	A good friend called me a neurotic person.	1	2	3	4	5
G.	I heard that my neighbor's son had an accident.	1	2	3	4	5
H.	My parents once accused me of being a failure in life.	1	2	3	4	5
I.	I recently spent a large sum of money on something I now think was a waste.	1	2	3	4	5
J.	Sometimes my kids tell me that I'm not a good parent.	1	2	3	4	5

Scoring: Tally the numbers you circle for the ten statements.

Score: re:

1-10	You are insensitive not only to other people's needs, but to your own.
11-20	You lead your life with a certain flair. There are probably not too many situations which will slow you down. You get along with people enough to promote yourself, and are somewhat insensitive to others.
21-30	You are concerned with other people's affairs as well as aware of your own feelings. Your flexibility in demanding situations may be helpful in preventing your becoming incapacitated by bad news and everyday difficulties.
31-40	You are a very sensitive person. It might be a good idea to reread all the statements to see whether there are any situations in which you're affected more than you would want.
41-50	You are apparently oversensitive to yourself and others. There are probably too many situations in your life in which the negatives outweigh the positives.

How High Is Up?

Answer the following statements by circling the number which describes most accurately your mood as affected by the described situations.

1. I feel deliriously happy.
2. I feel very happy.
3. I feel happy.
4. I don't feel happy.
5. I don't feel happy at all.

		1	2	3	4	5
A.	I discovered that I have more money in my wallet than I expected.	1	2	3	4	5
B.	I heard that my friend's sick child got well.	1	2	3	4	5
C.	My old mother has never been in such good health as now.	1	2	3	4	5
D.	Usually I don't spend money on myself, but I just bought something I really like.	1	2	3	4	5
E.	I am at the point of a very good relationship with my spouse.	1	2	3	4	5
F.	I was always the wonder-child in my family.	1	2	3	4	5
G.	This year my kids really expressed their love for me on Mother's (Father's) Day.	1	2	3	4	5
H.	My friends recognize my mental and emotional stability.	1	2	3	4	5
I.	I just made up with a good friend.	1	2	3	4	5
J.	I was just told that I'm in for a raise in salary.	1	2	3	4	5

Scoring: Figure out the score difference between the pairs of statements as indicated below. (Example: If you scored 5 on Statement A of Test 2 and scored 2 on Statement I of Test 3, the difference score is 3). Then tally all the difference scores.

The pairs are:

Blue Mood Barometer	How High Is Up?	Difference
A	I	
B	J	
C	C	
D	E	
E	A	
F	H	
G	B	
H	F	
I	D	
J	G	

Total score _____

Difference score:

1-10   Your mood remains very stable across different situations, a sign of emotional maturity.

11-20   You experience mood changes but do not generally allow them to disrupt your life. When you are happy you feel exuberant, but when sad, you try to keep it to yourself.

21-30   You tend to be somewhat moody. You have to make an effort not to allow your moods to adversely affect your personal relations.

31-40   Your mercurial shifts in mood are probably making life difficult for you. Try to see the differences between you and other people. Are you too dependent on them? Unassertive?

Emotional Compatibility

This test will help you determine to what degree you and your mate tolerate each other's habits and behavior. Answer each item by circling one of the numbers. Without showing your choices to your mate, let him/her complete the same test.

		Satisfied with Mate's Behavior		Not Sure		Dissatisfied with Mate's Behavior	
1. The way he/she eats	1	2	3	4	5	6	7
2. The way he/she talks	1	2	3	4	5	6	7
3. The way he/she dresses	1	2	3	4	5	6	7
4. How often he/she washes	1	2	3	4	5	6	7
5. The way he/she spends money	1	2	3	4	5	6	7
6. The way he/she undresses	1	2	3	4	5	6	7
7. The way he/she responds to lovemaking	1	2	3	4	5	6	7
8. The way he/she deals with others	1	2	3	4	5	6	7
9. The way he/she expresses emotions	1	2	3	4	5	6	7
10. The way he/she feels about you	1	2	3	4	5	6	7

Scoring: Tally each of your scores separately. Now subtract the lower score from the higher score to arrive at your difference score.

Difference score: 0-19   You both agree that you are either very happy or very unhappy together.

20-34   You have different opinions, but you're not too far apart. You ought to talk about these differences to one another. The more "not sure" answers you have, the more useful talking will be.

35-60   The differences between you are quite large. This could have been caused by a break down in communication between you. Obviously, if only one partner is dissatisfied, his/her complaints should be aired.

What Kind of Drinker Are You?

When drinking alcoholic beverages, to what degree do you experience the following responses? Check one category for each emotion.

		1 Never	2 Rarely	3 Sometimes	4 Frequently	5 Almost Always
A.	Friendly	____	____	____	____	____
B.	Depressed	____	____	____	____	____
C.	Excited	____	____	____	____	____
D.	Withdrawn	____	____	____	____	____
E.	Relaxed	____	____	____	____	____
F.	Frustrated	____	____	____	____	____
G.	Sexy	____	____	____	____	____
H.	Nervous	____	____	____	____	____
I.	Happy	____	____	____	____	____
J.	Detached	____	____	____	____	____
K.	Mentally Slow	____	____	____	____	____
L.	Guilty	____	____	____	____	____
M.	Angry	____	____	____	____	____

Scoring: Each checkmark scores the number of points indicated on top of the column. Break the list of responses into groups as follows and tally the points for each group.

Group I: A, E, G, I
Group II: B, D, J, K
Group III: C, F, H, M
Group IV: B, F, L, M

Score:

Group I   13-20   Have fun while it lasts. You are good company when drinking. If you overdo it, however, you may have problems staying vertical.

4-12   Consider other sources of entertainment besides those involving alcohol.

Group II   13-20   Drinking obviously brings out unpleasant feelings you have about yourself. This is not uncommon, but why go into a funk? Try drinking less.

4-12   Drinking doesn't seem to make you unsociable or morose.

Group III 13-20   You may be somewhat dangerous when you drink. In this state you may cause harm to others as well as to yourself. So carefully limit the quantity you drink.

4-12   It is possible to use the arousing effect of alcohol for more pleasant experiences. Try to work on yourself to move into Group I.

Group IV   13-20   Drink with people you like and trust. Better yet, don't drink. In your angry and depressed mood, you might say or do something to alienate your friends.

4-12   Drinking doesn't seem to trigger paranoia in you.

Your Range of Moods

This test will determine whether your mood changes a great deal, or whether it is stable. Read each stimulus word as fast as possible and equally fast write down next to it one association word from the following list. Before you start, read over the association words carefully at least twice!

Association Words

scary	effortless
nice	annoying
beautiful	friendly
stupid	reassuring
cruel	warm
simple	cold
calm	blinding
devious	sticky
sick	dominant
improper	clever
pleasant	angry
bugging	apathetic
good	relaxing
painful	demanding
super	dependent
swell	suffocating
grating	polite
obnoxious	secure
quiet	helpful
bad	bright
accommodating	knowledgeable

Stimulus Words

city —
dog —
boyfriend —
girl friend —
mother —
mayor —
boss —
father —
accident —
petting (necking) —
bus driver —
boss —
party (with many people) —
gas station attendant —
sexual intercourse —
surgery —
daughter —

son —

policeman —

grocer —

mugging —

blackout —

job —

letter carrier —

office —

medical checkup —

scuffle —

party (with few people) —

rape —

doctor —

cat —

Scoring: Use the key below to determine the number of pluses and minuses you collected. The closer the total is to zero, the more variable your mood is. The higher the score (net total of pluses or minuses), the more consistent your mood is, either in positive or negative situations. A low score indicates mood inconsistency.

Word	Value	Word	Value
scary	–	effortless	+
nice	+	annoying	–
beautiful	+	friendly	+
stupid	–	reassuring	+
cruel	–	warm	+
simple	+	cold	–
calm	+	blinding	–
devious	–	sticky	–
sick	–	dominant	–
improper	–	clever	+
pleasant	+	angry	–
bugging	–	apathetic	–
good	+	relaxing	+
painful	–	demanding	–
super	+	dependent	–
swell	+	suffocating	–
grating	–	polite	+
obnoxious	–	secure	+
quiet	+	helpful	+
bad	–	bright	+
accommodating	+	knowledgeable	+

Interpretation of Report Card Scores

"Color me" Test

Each of us reacts differently under varying circumstances. This test gives you an idea of your predominant emotional reaction pattern to certain critical situations.

Blue Mood Barometer

If you think you suffer excessive emotional pain, this test will give you some objective measurement of your distress.

How High Is Up?

This test assesses the stability of your moods. If you score high on this test, you should believe it when you are accused of being overly sensitive. A low score indicates emotional maturity.

Emotional Compatibility Test

How well do you know your mate? This test should give you a good idea of your emotional sensitivity to the person whose life you share.

What Kind of Drinker Are You?

Since alcohol lifts inhibitions and reveals underlying moods, this test gives you a good way to predict what you are apt to be like when you have had too much to drink. You will notice that some people's reactions to alcohol unearth frankly dangerous tendencies which should encourage strict sobriety.

Group I: Drinking brings out your sociable tendencies. Remember not to overdo it, since you possess the skill to be liked by others and shouldn't risk jeopardizing it.

Group II: Drinking gets you down on yourself.

Group III: You become aggressive and possibly even dangerous when you drink.

Group IV: You become overly suspicious when inebriated.

Your Range of Moods

This test can give three possible results:
High Positive = Optimistic
High Negative = Pessimistic
Low Score = Inconsistent or unpredictable mood

Test Results

Warren was a top salesman and, somewhat unusually for his profession, was able to maintain a close relationship with his wife despite his long absences from home. While on the road, however, due to loneliness and sometimes for business necessity, he drank too much. Each time this occurred he became extremely negative and insecure about himself. He would call his wife long-distance after having a few drinks, seeking reassurance and predicting his own failure. Needless to say, his wife became distraught after each phone call, thinking that Warren was encountering serious business difficulties or becoming depressed. After each trip, she would try to discuss his disturbing phone calls. He dismissed her concern as exaggerated. Finally, his drinking became more of a problem, especially when traveling — becoming noticeable to his colleagues and clients.

Warren had developed a pattern of drinking, common to many alcoholics, of becoming insecure under the influence of alcohol, and then drinking more in an effort to blot out those feelings. If you examine his test results below, you will see why he got into this dangerous rut and why he sought professional help to break the pattern.

Now fill in your own report card. Do you see better now why you react emotionally as you do?

Report Card for Moodiness

Warren Carson, Salesman

Tests	Low		Medium		High	
Blue Mood Barometer	1	15	16 ✶ 34		35	50
How High Is Up?	1 ✶ 13		14	37	28	40
Emotional Compatibility Test	0 ✶ 19		21	34	35	60
What Kind of Drinker Are You?						
Group I	4 ✶ 9		10	15	16	20
Group II	4	9	10	15	16 ✶ 20	
Group III	4 ✶ 9		10	15	16	20
Group IV	4 ✶ 9		10	15	16	20
Your Range of Moods	±21 ✶ ±15		±14 ⋮ ± 7		± 6	0

Instructions: Go back to each of the tests included in this report card and transfer your score by placing an X on the score you obtained. Your overall standing will be indicated by where the majority of the X symbols are placed.

Report Card for Moodiness

Tests	Low		Medium		High	
Blue Mood Barometer	1	15	16	34	35	50
How High Is Up?	1	13	14	27	28	40
Emotional Compatibility Test	0	19	21	34	35	60
What Kind of Drinker Are You?						
Group I	4	9	10	15	16	20
Group II	4	9	10	15	16	20
Group III	4	9	10	15	16	20
Group IV	4	9	10	15	16	20
Your Range of Moods	±21	±15	±14	±7	± 6	0

6 Are You a Survivor?

Each morning as you brush your teeth, you see a familiar face in the mirror — your own. Behind that face is a personality, perhaps not as familiar to you as it should be.

Personality is an aggregate of your style of thinking, interacting, and responding emotionally. It rarely varies after it receives its final shaping in the adolescent years, and yet many people lack familiarity with their own personality tendencies.

"I didn't know I was coming on so strong" is a statement by someone unfamiliar with his or her ability to intimidate others.

A statement such as "Somehow he just turned off to me" reflects a blind spot in the perception of one's own personality traits that act as a turn-off to others.

While there are many ways to measure and assess personality, one critical aspect of the way you function is whether or not your typical emotional responses and style of interacting will serve you well when the chips are down — when you are in a crisis and the only survival resource you have at your disposal is your personality. The tests in this chapter measure certain functions of personality that have been found by clinicians to be associated with people who have excellent survival skills. It's important to review the test results summarized in the report card at the end of the chapter and pinpoint those areas of personality functioning in which you are weak. This will give you valuable information in terms of strengthening your ways of coping with situations so that you can develop a reliable and durable survivor type of personality.

Self-directed/Other-directed

Completion of this test will help you to get to know yourself better. Read each item and circle the sentence with which you agree more strongly.

1. (a) When I want to get somewhere on time I need only plan to get the bus, train, or plane on time.
   (b) Since I never can rely on buses, trains, or planes to keep to their schedules, I must have contingency plans ready to make sure I get to where I'm going on time.

2. (a) If I had a dog, I could train it to be obedient and friendly.
   (b) A dog's susceptibility to training depends primarily on its breed.

3. (a) Successful cooking means simply following the recipe.
   (b) Successful cooking means being imaginative in the kitchen.

4. (a) I don't mind if my neighbor (whom I see frequently) is in a nasty mood.
   (b) It is so nice to have pleasant people around oneself.

5. (a) Balancing my household budget depends on how much my family eats.
   (b) One can save money by careful planning of expenditures.

6. (a) Happiness can be defined as a "gut feeling" of calm and satisfaction.
   (b) Happiness is a child's smile.

7. (a) Prevention of crime depends on everybody's willingness to fight it together.
   (b) The only way not to become a crime victim is to look over one's shoulder.

8. (a) Decisions which are made in a group are the most valid.
   (b) The most efficient way of getting on in life is by being decisive.

9. (a) It is up to society to take care of invalids and cripples.
   (b) Even a blind amputee can learn to write a letter if he wants to badly enough.

10. (a) Most millionaires worked hard to get to where they are.
    (b) Society favors some people and not others.

11. (a) Being a good citizen requires you to be attentive to the media's daily reports.
    (b) Being a good citizen means keeping one's own house in order.

12. (a) Religion is a good thing for mankind.
    (b) One's fate is determined mainly by one's own actions.

13. (a) A candlelight dinner for two is my speed.
    (b) I like going to big parties on New Year's Eve.

14. (a) I prefer to have at least two mirrors in my house.
    (b) The moral in the Snow White fairy tale is an important one.

Scoring: Score 1 point for each answer according to the answer key below. Your score is a measure of the degree to which you are influenced by others rather than by your own convictions. If your score is low, you are more self-directed than other-directed.

1. (a)	5. (a)	8. (a)	12. (a)
2. (b)	6. (b)	9. (a)	13. (b)
3. (a)	7. (a)	10. (b)	14. (a)
4. (b)		11. (a)	

In Figure A, embellish the drawing of the house. In Figure B, count how many triangles there are in the pattern.

FIGURE A

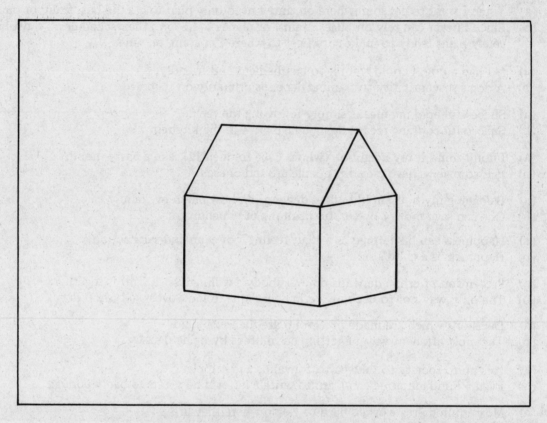

FIGURE B

Scoring: If you drew objects outside the frame of the house (Figure A) you are relatively unaffected by predominant stimuli in your environment. You act more freely than a person who "sticks to the frame." If you counted eight triangles (Figure B), you are relatively unaffected by distractions and can concentrate on an important task.

How Do You See Yourself/Others?

Look at Picture 1 carefully. Examine every detail and try to imagine what is happening in the scene depicted. Then complete the story for Picture 1 by filling the blanks with words chosen from the list on page 84. Try to identify with one of the people in the pictures.

PICTURE 1

Story for Picture 1

The man in the picture seems to be a *respectful* lawyer. The woman is a *liberated* secretary. In personality the man seems to be *quiet*, while the woman is probably a *aggressive* person. They have just been talking about their relationship. She said she needed more *independence* from him, while he said he wanted more *affection* from her. The lawyer said he would like to be more ___, while the secretary said she would aim to be more ___. In his work the man feels ___, and the woman feels ___ in her job. They have known each other for quite a long time, being mostly ___ toward (of) each other. Basically they ___ each other and would like to ___. More often than not they "pleasantly accuse" one another of being too ___. Each agreed, however, to work on his or her end of the deal. It is difficult to predict, but most people in their situation end up becoming ___ in their relationship.

Follow the same instructions as For Picture 1.

Story for Picture 2

The person in the picture is thinking of something that has just happened. He/she has a/an ____ friend
16
whom he/she has known for a long time. Yesterday, after going with this friend to the movies, the
friend said that ____ friends cannot go on like this for a long time. It is true that recently he/she felt
17
____ toward the friend. Afraid that their relationship would turn ____ , it was decided to talk to the
18   19
friend and ask to try to be more ____ . Behaving in a ____ way toward one another may ____ the
20   21   22
respect between them. The person in the picture imagines that the friend's reaction to all this will
be ____ . He/she doesn't feel ____ toward his/her friend.
   23   24

Word List for Filling the Blanks

sour	respect	clever	hates	warmth	disappointed
love	disdain	dominant	aggressive	independence	antagonistic
independent	considerate	hateful	successful	acknowledgment	obedient
reliable	bored	ruin	soft	sex	submissive
warm	bad	save	angry	sweet	weak
close	affectionate	lose	pushy	compliance	strong
cold	loud	accepting	incompetent	separate	liberated
detached	dependent	rejecting	respectful	understanding	quiet
remote	humiliating	indifference	marry	happy	
affair	deficient	loves	can't stand	hostile	
compulsive	freedom	individualistic	conforming	satisfied	

Scoring: In order to understand your score on this test, you have to be slightly imaginative. Basically, your responses fall into two categories: (1) how you perceive yourself in interactions, and (2) how you perceive others who interact with you (or your perception of your relationship). Thus in the scoring it makes a difference whether you are male or female.

For females:	Perception of self	Blanks number 2,4,5,8,10,21,22,24
	Perception of other	Blanks number 1,3,11,12,13,14,15,16,17,18,19,20,21,22,23
For males:	Perception of self	Blanks number 1,3,7,9,12,13,24
	Perception of other	Blanks number 2,4,6,11,12,13,14,15,16,17,18,19,20,21,22,23

The words on the list fall into four categories:

Angry/aggressive   sour, cold, detached, remote, disdainful, bored, bad, loud, humiliating, hateful, rejecting, indifference, hates, aggressive, angry, pushy, can't stand, hostile, antagonistic

Warm/accepting   love, affair, respect, considerate, affectionate, save, accepting, loves, soft, respectful, marry, warmth, acknowledgment, sweet, understanding, happy

Dependence   reliable, dependent, ruin, lose, incompetent, conforming, compliance, disappointed, obedient, submissive, weak, quiet

Independence   independent, warm, close, compulsive, efficient, freedom, clever, dominant, individualistic, successful, independence, separate, satisfied, strong, liberated

By checking which words you used for filling in the blanks, you will be able to discern in what light you see yourself and your relationships with others.

Note: This test is not designed to assess your personality or your partner's personality. Its purpose is to start you thinking about your feelings concerning yourself and others.

Outgoing/Withdrawn

This test will determine just how involved you are with your environment. Read each question, then circle one of the replies.

(A) You just noticed a new neighbor moving into the apartment below you. Would you

1. Nod to him as you pass by?
2. Send him a welcome card?
3. Go speak to him and offer your help?

(B) A group of children are taunting a little dog. Would you

1. Ignore it?
2. Tell the children to stop?
3. Take the dog to the SPCA?

(C) You are at a New Year's Eve party. Someone begins to sing. Would you

1. Just look on?
2. Hum with the tune?
3. Sing out loud with everybody?

(D) You are sitting in a waiting room of the dentist's office. Other patients look at you. Would you

1. Smile at them?
2. Make up stories about them?
3. Ask them questions?

(E) Your circle of friends would like to have a party. Would you

1. Agree that it is a good idea?
2. Offer to help organize it?
3. Offer to have the party at your home?

(F) When drinking alcoholic beverages do you

1. Become more withdrawn?
2. Feel generally unchanged?
3. Become more friendly and talkative?

(G) The grocer asks how you intend to use the yeast you just bought. Would you

1. Smile and not say anything?
2. Say that it is for a cake?
3. Tell him more about the cake recipe?

(H) You have just witnessed a minor car accident. Would you

1. Just walk on?
2. Stop and see what the drivers do?
3. Go over and offer to be a witness?

(I) In a discussion group someone just expressed an opinion you strongly disagree with. Would you

1. Ignore it, feeling the person is stupid?
2. Say to him "You are wrong"?
3. Try to convince the group of your opinion?

(J)   You are about to meet a new date. Would you

1.   Wait to see what your partner wants to do?
2.   Plan some entertainment?
3.   Decide on a plan and hope your partner agrees with it?

Scoring: Tally your score by totaling the numbers you circled (1, 2, or 3 points).

Score: 24-30   You are very outgoing, involved, and ready to play a role in your community.

17-23   Your involvement is about average for the American urban citizen.

10-16   You tend to be withdrawn.

Optimistic/Pessimistic

This test will help you determine whether or not you are an optimist regarding your life. Read each item and circle the opinion with which you agree most strongly.

1. (a)   The economic situation in the world would improve if people changed their consumption style.
    (b)   Sooner or later the world (or most of it) will turn Communist.

2. (a)   No world leader can do anything about starvation in India.
    (b)   Starvation in India can be cured by birth control programs.

3. (a)   My interaction with my friends satisfies me.
    (b)   I do not have enough friends.

4. (a)   The weather forecast is usually accurate in the summer.
    (b)   No matter what the forecast is, it is safer to take an umbrella.

5. (a)   My political party will not win the presidency in the next election.
    (b)   I've been lucky to stick with the party that will win each time.

6. (a)   When I hear a loud noise at night I first think it is a burglar.
    (b)   When I hear a loud noise at night I first think it is a neighbor slamming his door.

7. (a)   I would like to have a fire alarm in my house.
    (b)   I am very nervous about the possibility of fire breaking out in my house.

8. (a)   When my date is late I blame him/her.
    (b)   When my date is late I blame the bus.

9. (a)   When I see my bus at the bus stop I usually run a few steps to catch it.
    (b)   When I see my bus at the bus stop I usually keep on walking at the same pace.

10. (a)   People usually lose 38 percent of their hair by the age of fifty-seven.
     (b)   Some people become bald under severe stress.

Scoring: Check your answers against the answer key below. Score 1 point as indicated for each answer. The higher your score, the more optimistic and self-reliant you are.

1.	(a)	6.	(b)
2.	(b)	7.	(a)
3.	(a)	8.	(b)
4.	(a)	9.	(b)
5.	(b)	10.	(a)

How Deep Is Your Rut?

This test will tell you how important routine and order are for you in your everyday life. Circle one answer for each statement.

		Always	Usually	Seldom
1.	I get up at the same time every morning.	A	B	C
2.	I eat lunch at the same place every day.	A	B	C
3.	I like to vary the newspapers I read.	A	B	C
4.	I get hungry at the same time before lunch.	A	B	C
5.	I don't care if my hair isn't combed.	A	B	C
6.	I don't recheck to see if I locked my door before leaving.	A	B	C
7.	I always affix a stamp right side up on an envelope.	A	B	C
8.	When writing a letter on lined paper I write "double space."	A	B	C
9.	I don't carry a handkerchief with me.	A	B	C
10.	I have identification papers on me.	A	B	C
11.	I wash my car regularly.	A	B	C
12.	I like to write with a pencil regardless of whether it has a sharp point.	A	B	C
13.	I call a friend on the phone to make sure he's home before I go there.	A	B	C
14.	I estimate the time when I boil an egg.	A	B	C

Scoring:

> For statements 1,2,4,7,10,11,13:   A = 3 points; B = 2 points; C = 1 point.
> For statements 3,5,6,8,9,12,14:   A = 1 point; B = 2 points; C = 3 points.

The higher your total score, the more compulsive, organized, and rigid you are.

Self-Confidence Test

Answer the following questions to find out how confident you are in your performance in various situations.

		Yes	No
1.	When I see two people quarreling, I try to stop them.		
2.	I am an excellent driver.		
3.	If I saw a cop chasing a pickpocket, I would help the cop.		
4.	I can succeed in getting most jobs I apply for.		
5.	If my boss asked me to take his place temporarily, I would.		
6.	I can impress any stranger I'm introduced to.		
7.	If I saw a person shoplifting, I'd report him/her.		
8.	I can deliver a speech before a large audience.		
9.	I can tell a person not to cut in line in front of me.		

10. In case of a fire I would help elderly people out of the burning building.

11. If I set my mind to it, I can be successful.

12. I believe if you scratch the surface you will find greed in everybody.

Scoring: Score 1 point for each No answer, and 2 points for each Yes.

Score: 12-15   Low self-confidence
      16-19   Average self-confidence
      20-24   High self-confidence

Rigidity-Flexibility Test

This test is designed to determine how you are affected by unexpected changes in your plans, and whether you adapt well. Answer each item by circling the appropriate number.

	Not at All	A Little	Quite	Very
1. How upset do you get when your mate does not arrive on time?	1	2	3	4
2. How disturbed are you when the movie you have tickets for is delayed by half an hour?	1	2	3	4
3. How annoyed are you when your plane's departure time has been delayed by two hours?	1	2	3	4
4. How disappointed are you when an invited friend cancels out?	1	2	3	4
5. How disappointed are you when you find out that the sale you intended to take advantage of is over?	1	2	3	4
6. How angry do you get when your bus leaves fifteen seconds before you get to the stop?	1	2	3	4
7. How upset do you get when your kids who were told to clean the kitchen did not do so?	1	2	3	4
8. How upset do you get when you find out that the cleaner sent you someone else's clothing?	1	2	3	4
9. How annoyed do you get when you discover that your car has not been fixed as promised?	1	2	3	4
10. How disappointed do you get upon finding that the price of an object you intended to buy has just been raised?	1	2	3	4
11. How upset do you get when a party you've been invited to is canceled?	1	2	3	4
12. How annoyed do you get when your morning newspaper hasn't been delivered?	1	2	3	4

Scoring: Tally the numbers you circled.

Score: 12-23   You are a flexible person and don't get thrown if things change unexpectedly.

       24-35   You are annoyed by some unexpected surprises but find that you can usually adapt.

       36-48   You are a rigid person and apparently hate it when things get out of your control.

Habit Test

This test is designed to determine whether you have certain strong habits.

                                                                    Yes   No

1. Do you look under your bed before you go to sleep at night?
2. Do you wash your hands even if you're certain they are clean?
3. Do you check your mailbox again after having checked previously?
4. Do you return home after you left, to check whether you have locked the back door?
5. Do you overwash your fruits or vegetables?
6. Do you make sure that there is no obstacle left on your stairs?
7. Do you always replace certain food staples before they are used up?
8. Do you overclean your home?
9. Do you wipe a public toilet seat before sitting down?
10. Do you always wash your hands after using the bathroom?
11. Do you wash the dirty dishes after each meal?
12. Do you look in the mirror often to make sure you look okay?
13. If you make a spelling mistake in the first sentence of a letter, do you toss it out and start a new sheet of paper?
14. Do you make sure the stove is off before leaving your home?
15. Do you always wash before making love?
16. Do you clean your desk before beginning to work?

Scoring: Score 1 point for each No answer.

Score: 11-16   You are not in a habit rut.

       6-10   You are a slightly overcautious person worried about making a wrong move and suffering the consequences.

       1-5   You are a worried person, probably very rigid and continually thinking about dire consequences. Some consider this behavior characteristic of an obsessive-compulsive personality.

Interpretation of Report Card Scores

Self-directed/Other-directed	This test measures the degree to which you rely on your own judgment and convictions.
Stimulus-bound/Stimulus-free	This test indicates whether or not you are able to set aside convention in order to find a solution.
How Do You See Yourself/Others?	This test assesses four characteristics: aggressiveness, acceptance, dependence, and independence. A survivor personality would be low on anger/aggressiveness (learning not to make waves in order to survive); high on acceptance, ensuring inclusion in any group; low on dependence and high on independence, for obvious reasons.
Outgoing/Withdrawn	Clearly, the more outgoing, the more likely one is to explore new avenues for survival.
Optimistic/Pessimistic	For survival to mean anything, one must believe there will be a good future. Otherwise, why struggle so hard to keep going?
How Deep Is Your Rut?	If you are programed to keep going in one direction only, some day you will go off the edge of a cliff. A survivor must always eye the road ahead, taking detours whenever necessary.
Self-Confidence Test	Belief in your abilities is one of the key ingredients for survival under adverse circumstances.
Rigidity/Flexibility Test and Habit Test	These two tests combined give you some indication of your ability to roll with the punches. You must be able to accept constant change if you are to survive in a crisis. You must also be willing to suspend habit patterns for the sake of making it through a difficult situation.

Test Results

Judy's husband just walked out on her to go live with a twenty-three-year-old woman he had met at work. Judy was hurt when he confessed about his affair and revealed his decision to "try to make a new life with Charlotte." Her confidence in herself had suffered for a while as she considered the warnings of her friends. "There's nothing out there. Why don't you fight to keep him, even if you have to make him feel guilty for leaving the kids at such a young age?" Judy declined to heed their warnings. She's making out just fine now. Can you guess why by reviewing her Survivor Personality Report Card?

Now fill in your test results and see what kind of survivor you would be in a crisis.

Report Card for Survivor Personality

Judy DeCaprio, Teacher

Tests	Low		Medium		High	
Self-directed/Other-directed	0	4	5	8	9	✱ 15
Stimulus-bound/Stimulus-free						
Figure A	0	2	3	4	5	✱ +
Figure B	0	2	3	4	5 ✱	8
How Do You See Yourself/Others?						
Angry/aggressive	21	16	15 ✱	8	7	0
Warm/accepting	0	5	6 ✱	10	11	16
Dependence	12	9	8	5	4 ✱	0
Independence	0	5	6	10	11	✱ 15
Outgoing/Withdrawn	10	16	17	23	24	✱ 30
Optimistic/Pessimistic	0	3	4	6	7	✱ 10
How Deep Is Your Rut?	42	34	33 ✱	24	23	14
Self-Confidence Test	12	15	16 ✱	19	20	24
Rigidity/Flexibility Test	48	36	35	24	23	✱ 12
Habit Test	1	5	6	10	11	✱ 16

Instructions: Go back to each of the tests included in this report card and transfer your score by placing an X on the score you obtained. Your overall standing will be indicated by where the majority of the X symbols are placed.

Report Card for Survivor Personality

Tests	Low		Medium		High	
Self-directed/Other-directed	0	4	5	8	9	15
Stimulus-bound/Stimulus-free						
Figure A	0	2	3	4	5	+
Figure B	0	2	3	4	5	8
How Do You See Yourself/Others?						
Angry/aggressive	21	16	15	8	7	0
Warm/accepting	0	5	6	10	11	16
Dependence	12	9	8	5	4	0
Independence	0	5	6	10	11	15
Outgoing/Withdrawn	10	16	17	23	24	30
Optimistic/Pessimistic	0	3	4	6	7	10
How Deep Is Your Rut?	42	34	33	24	23	14
Self-Confidence Test	12	15	16	19	20	24
Rigidity/Flexibility Test	48	36	35	24	23	12
Habit Test	1	5	6	10	11	16

7 Are You a Good Friend, Lover, Etc.?

There is no area of life that causes more grief and yet is responsible for more satisfactions than the relationships we have with others. Despite prophecies of the destruction of the family unit, young people continue to get married and divorced people continue to remarry in steadily growing numbers. The discouraging side of the statistical picture is that divorces occur in fully 38 percent of all marriages and, if one considers second marriages, that figure rises to 44 percent. Quite clearly, many people have serious difficulties in interpersonal relationships. That fact should not surprise anyone. The human being is an extremely complex entity composed of attitudes, needs, biases, capacities, deficiencies, etc.

No one is an open book, and others know only as much about you as you choose to reveal. Even if you are an extremely forthright and honest person, how others perceive you may be colored by their own biases and neurotic traits. We are taught to compensate for these deficiencies by "clear communications," but what is that? In any communication, there is a sender and a receiver. If you wish to have good relationships, you must learn to be a good communicator — that is, a good sender and a good receiver, or a good talker and a good listener.

In this chapter you will be tested on certain capacities that are known to be associated with people who are skilled in interpersonal relationships. The test results enable you to pinpoint which areas of your interpersonal skills require strengthening. The report card at the end of the chapter will provide a profile of your interpersonal relationships in a qualitative way. It would be an excellent idea if you reread this chapter after a few months and retook the tests in order to chart your progress as a communicator.

The Dual Morality Standard Test

Read each question and circle the appropriate answer. Your answers to these questions should tell you how you react in different situations.

A. As you walk down a street, you see a driver sideswipe a parked car. Would you

    1. Keep on walking?
    2. Take down the driver's license number?
    3. Ask the driver for the name of his insurance company?

B. You notice a group of kids light a fire in a yard. Would you

    1. Not interfere?
    2. Tell the kids to put out the fire?
    3. Bring water and extinguish the fire yourself?

C. If you were told that smoking will increase your chances of getting cancer, would you

1. Pay no heed?
2. Reduce the amount you smoke?
3. Quit smoking immediately?

D. When you don't feel well in the morning, do you

1. Stay in bed?
2. Get up but stay home that day?
3. Go to work in spite of how you feel?

E. When you see a driver in trouble on the highway, do you

1. Pass him?
2. Report the problem to the highway patrol?
3. Stop and offer help?

F. You are a witness to a rape. Would you

1. Do nothing?
2. Call the cops?
3. Try to stop the attack?

G. When your child disobeys you, do you

1. Pay no attention?
2. Warn him to obey?
3. Slap him and tell him what to do?

H. When you know someone is lying to you, do you

1. Let it pass unmentioned?
2. Tell him you know he's lying?
3. Sever your relationship with him?

I. Your income this past year has increased. Would you

1. Not report the increase to the income tax authorities?
2. Report part of the increase?
3. Report the entire increase?

J. Circle the statement you believe in most:

1. It is good for me to be lazy.
2. It is good for me to be lazy sometimes.
3. It is never good for me to be lazy.

Scoring: For the moment, just think about your answers. What do you conclude about your behavior and attitudes in the above described situations? Now go on to the next test.

Judgment of Others

Read each question and circle the appropriate answer. Your answer to these questions should tell you what you think others should do . . . and something else too.

A. Someone tells you he was cheated in a game by his friend. Would you advise him to

  1. Forget about it?
  2. Confront his friend?
  3. Look for a new friend?

B. Your neighbor saw an old woman being mugged. Do you think he should have

  1. Done nothing?
  2. Called for help?
  3. Gone over to save the woman?

C. A friend noticed that the bank credited her account by mistake. Do you think she should

  1. Pocket the money?
  2. Report that a smaller than actual mistake has been made?
  3. Tell the bank manager about the whole sum?

D. A friend tells you he just saw someone accidently crack a store's glass door. Would you advise him

  1. Not to get involved?
  2. To take the person's description?
  3. To ask the person for his I.D.?

E. When a teacher has trouble with one of her pupils, should she

  1. Ignore him?
  2. Tell him to shape up?
  3. Use physical punishment in order to restrain him?

F. If a bystander sees a group of youngsters playing with unattended construction equipment, should he

  1. Let them do what they want?
  2. Tell them to go home?
  3. Chase them away?

G. How should a hiker in the mountains behave when he sees someone in trouble across a small brook?

  1. Not get involved.
  2. Tell the forest ranger about it.
  3. Cross the brook and offer help.

H. A person who has a bad cold should

  1. Take medication and stay in bed.
  2. Take medication and stay home working.
  3. Take medication and go about his business as usual.

I. A friend of yours was told by his doctor that if he continued to drink he would destroy his liver. Do you think he should

1. Forget about those medical people?
2. Drink less?
3. Stop drinking?

J. Circle the statement you believe in most:

1. Young people should have lots of leisure.
2. Young people should work as well as have fun.
3. Young people should be always busy and productive.

Scoring: Determine the difference score for the following item pairs (the first is from this test, the second from the preceding test). Subtract the lower score from the higher one (e.g., if you scored 3 on item J in this test and 2 on item J on the preceding test, your difference score is 1). Tally your 10 difference scores. If you score between 10 and 20, it means that you hold a different set of values for others than for yourself. If you score 0 to 10, you would be likely to advise others to do what you yourself would do in certain situations.

Pairs: A-H;   B-F;   C-I;   D-A;   E-G;   F-B;   G-E;   H-D;   I-C;   J-J.

Assertiveness

This test will assess your ability to stand up for your rights in different situations. Answer each statement by choosing one of the following numbers: 1 = Does not describe me; 2 = Describes me somewhat; 3 = Very descriptive of me.

	Not Me	Sometimes Me	Always Me
1. I look at a person's eyes when I talk to him.	1	2	3
2. People do not have difficulty hearing me when I speak.	1	2	3
3. I don't mind asking friends to lend me money.	1	2	3
4. I talk to strangers on the bus.	1	2	3
5. I go to stores to exchange faulty merchandise.	1	2	3
6. I complain to the waiter if I'm made to wait a long time.	1	2	3
7. I tell people when I disagree with them.	1	2	3
8. I don't mind going with someone I know to visit a stranger.	1	2	3
9. I protest when I'm not served in my turn.	1	2	3
10. I make sure nobody cuts in line in front of me.	1	2	3

	Not Me	Sometimes Me	Always Me
11. I tell people to obey "no smoking" signs.	1	2	3
12. I do not find it difficult to telephone people I don't know.	1	2	3
13. If a friend lets me down, I discuss it with him.	1	2	3
14. If someone damages property I lent to him, I make him repair or replace it.	1	2	3
15. I tell my spouse (partner) off when he/she bugs me.	1	2	3

Scoring: Tally the numbers you chose.

Score: 15-25   You are not particularly assertive.

26-35   You are in the average range of assertiveness.

36-45   You are very assertive and stand up for yourself when you feel you are in the right.

Dating

This test will tell you how good a "dater" you are. The test is mainly for single people, but if you are married, you can read the test and fantasize a bit. Answer each statement by choosing one of the following numbers: 1 = Does not describe me; 2 = Describes me somewhat; 3 = Very descriptive of me.

	Not Me	Sometimes Me	Always Me
1. I can call someone up for a blind date.	1	2	3
2. If I see a man/woman sitting alone at a table, I could go over and talk to him/her if I wanted to.	1	2	3
3. I talk to strangers of the opposite sex on the bus.	1	2	3
4. When I meet someone new, I do not get anxious at all.	1	2	3
5. If I and my new date are not enjoying the party we're at, I invite him/her to my place.	1	2	3
6. I dress to impress when I go on a date.	1	2	3
7. I look at my date's eyes when I talk to her/him.	1	2	3
8. I invite a new date to dinner.	1	2	3
9. I meet socially with someone from work.	1	2	3
10. If I see someone interesting at a party or meeting, I make the effort to get to know him/her better.	1	2	3

	Not Me	Sometimes Me	Always Me
11. If I'm attracted to someone, I'll go out of my way to meet her/him.	1	2	3
12. I date very often.	1	2	3

Scoring: Tally the numbers you circled.

Score:		
	12-20	Poor dating skills
	21-29	Average dating skills
	30-36	Good dating skills

How Do You Feel About Authority?

Answer the following statements by circling the number that best describes your opinion.

	Not At all	Some-what	Very Much
1. I respect policemen.	1	2	3
2. I always obeyed my mother.	1	2	3
3. I always obeyed my father.	1	2	3
4. I think laws are there to be enforced.	1	2	3
5. I would have liked to be an officer had I been in the Army.	1	2	3
6. My boss is very understanding.	1	2	3
7. Our mayor is very capable.	1	2	3
8. One should always pay one's taxes.	1	2	3
9. When they ask the public to conserve energy, I do my share.	1	2	3
10. I obey all traffic signs.	1	2	3
11. I think the army's uniform is beautiful.	1	2	3
12. I think doctors know a lot.	1	2	3
13. Obeying orders is the most efficient way to achieve progress within the establishment.	1	2	3

Scoring: Tally the numbers you circled.

Score:		
	13-21	You are not in awe of authority.
	22-29	Your relations with authority are ambivalent.
	30-39	You are very obedient and conformist.

Attitude Toward Your Children

For each of your children place an X on the line which would best describe the way you perceive that child.

1.	Kind	_____	Cruel
2.	Strong	_____	Weak
3.	Loving	_____	Hateful
4.	Smart	_____	Dumb
5.	Good	_____	Bad
6.	Coordinated	_____	Awkward
7.	Beautiful	_____	Ugly
8.	Warm	_____	Cold
9.	Honest	_____	Deceitful
10.	Independent	_____	Dependent

Scoring: It is assumed your perception of your child will reflect on your relationship with that child. For each of the ten items, take a ruler and measure from left to right. Add up the number of inches.

Score: 0-15" Generally you have a positive attitude toward your child. The lower the score, the more approvingly you view your child.

Above 15" You see your child in a negative light. The higher the score, the more disapproving your perception.

Relationship with Your Mate

This test will give you an idea of the nature of your relationship with your mate. Choose the answer that comes closest to describing your relationship.

1. My mate and I fight   (1) Never   (2) Sometimes   (3) Often
2. I love my mate   (1) Do not   (2) A little   (3) Very Much
3. We understand each other   (1) Seldom   (2) Often   (3) Always
4. We have sex   (1) Seldom   (2) Sometimes   (3) Often
5. We have the same taste   (1) Never   (2) In some things   (3) Always
6. We experience good things together   (1) Often   (2) Sometimes   (3) Rarely
7. We talk to each other a lot.   (1) No   (2) Average   (3) Yes
8. He/she respects me   (1) Yes   (2) Sometimes   (3) No
9. I respect him/her   (1) Yes   (2) Sometimes   (3) No
10. We disagree on things   (1) Never   (2) Sometimes   (3) Always
11. When apart, we miss each other   (1) Seldom   (2) Sometimes   (3) Often
12. We think about separating   (1) Often   (2) Sometimes   (3) Seldom
13. We share common interests   (1) Many   (2) A few   (3) None
14. When one is talking, the other interrupts   (1) Never   (2) Sometimes   (3) Always
15. If we have a problem, we discuss it   (1) Always   (2) Sometimes   (3) Never

Scoring:

For items 2, 3, 4, 5, 7, 11, 12, tally the numbers you circled.

For items 1, 6, 8, 9, 10, 13, 14, 15, reverse the point order (i.e., if you chose (1), score 3 points; if you chose (3), score 1; (2) remains 2).

Total score:
- 15-25   Poor to average relationship
- 26-35   Average to good relationship
- 36-45   Good to very good relationship

Color Test II (How You Feel About Others)

This test will reveal how you feel about members of the opposite sex. Males should color the five female figures; females should color the five male figures.

Males should imagine the figures to be: A date; a female boss; a female co-worker; a female stranger; a female family member.

Females should imagine the figures to be: A date; a male boss; a male co-worker; a male stranger; a male family member.

Using yellow, red, blue, and green pencils or felt-tip pens, color each figure completely.

DATE

BOSS

CO-WORKER

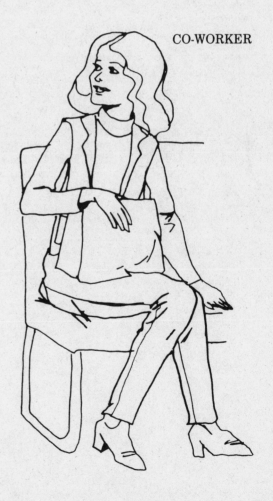

STRANGER

FAMILY MEMBER

DATE

BOSS

STRANGER

CO-WORKER

FAMILY MEMBER

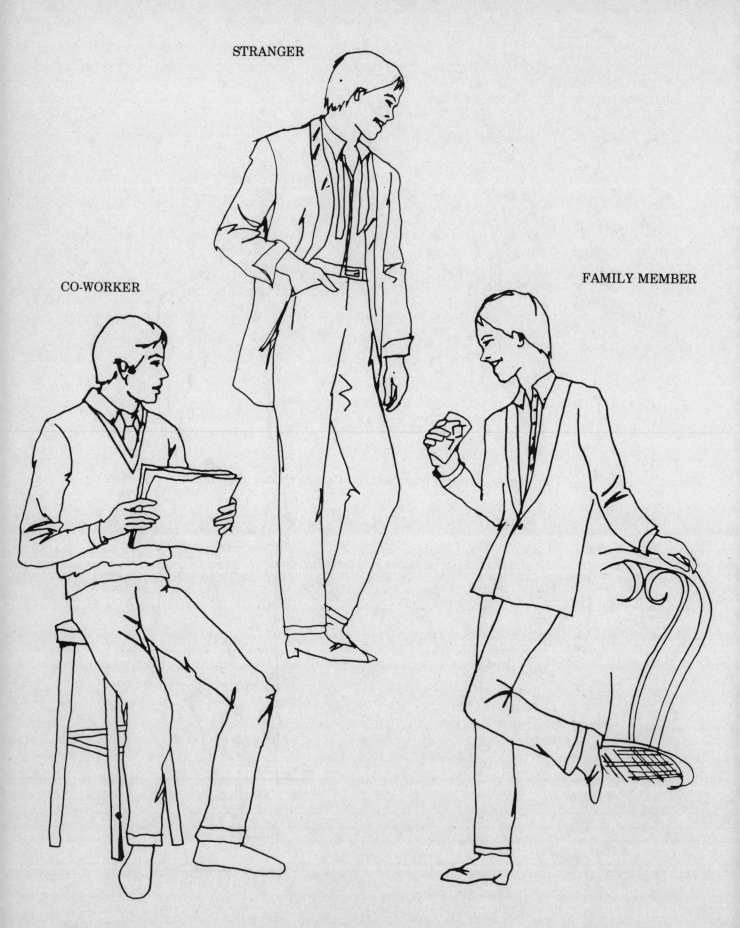

Scoring: As you did in the "Color Me" test in Chapter Five, determine the percentage of yellow, red, blue, and green you used for each figure. Each color is believed to represent an emotional tendency. Use the color key that follows to determine how you perceive each of the five persons you colored.

Hair –	5%
Face –	10%
Neck –	5%
Shirt, Blouse –	6%
Jacket, Sweater, Vest, Accessories (handbag, briefcase, etc.) –	25%
Arm R –	4%
Arm L –	4%
Hand R –	4%
Hand L –	4%
Belt –	5%
Pants, Skirt –	25%
Shoe R –	4%
Shoe L –	4%

Color Key:

Highest % yellow   You see this person of the opposite sex as interesting and sophisticated. He/she can be trusted in his/her judgment and decisions. This is an experienced and socially adept person. He/she is a good person to do things with but may be slightly impulsive.

Highest % red   This person is seen as impulsive and strong. He/she likes to get into a heated discussion and usually wins. This person is warm, exudes good spirits, and is affected by a show of affection. He/she is a giving person, helpful, and a good person to have on your side. He/she is slightly egocentric.

Highest % blue   This person in seen as usually quite relaxed and accepting, though at times cool and detached. He/she has an understanding nature and likes to help, yet is hesitant to make the first move. The initiative must come from elsewhere. At times he/she is somewhat oversensitive to others.

Highest % green   This person is seen as somewhat pushy and assertive. He/she may have a tendency to hurt others in the process, and does not like to be disagreed with. This person is self-confident and strong. His/her social interaction style isn't always smooth, and his/her relations with co-workers are somewhat stiff.

Who's Your Ideal Mate?

This test is designed to help you outline the characteristics you would want to find in an "ideal" mate. Answer each item by circling the appropriate number.

		Negative	Neutral	Positive
1.	To understand money matters	1	2	3
2.	To be a homebody	1	2	3
3.	To be a quiet person	1	2	3
4.	To like to go to movies	1	2	3
5.	To have studied something in depth	1	2	3
6.	To be talkative	1	2	3
7.	To be orderly	1	2	3
8.	To read newspapers	1	2	3
9.	To understand politics	1	2	3
10.	To like children	1	2	3
11.	To be able to pun	1	2	3
12.	To decorate your home	1	2	3
13.	To be sexy	1	2	3
14.	To eat out	1	2	3
15.	To know arithmetic	1	2	3
16.	To be affectionate	1	2	3
17.	To make money	1	2	3
18.	To have nice furniture	1	2	3
19.	To love plants	1	2	3
20.	To live freely without a schedule	1	2	3
21.	To be well read	1	2	3

Scoring:

Group A: for items 1, 5, 8, 9, 11, 15, 17, 21, tally the numbers you circled.

Score:
8-13   You are not too interested in a "brainy" person.

14-19   You are undecided about the importance of intellectual activities.

20-24   Mental capabilities are important to you.

Group B: for items 2, 4, 12, 14, 18, 19, tally the numbers you circled. For items 4 and 14, reverse the numbers (if you circled 1, score 3 points; if you circled 3, score 1 point; 2 remains the same) and add to score.

Score:
6-9   You believe in leading a life outside the home.

10-14   No strong opinion.

15-18   You like making your home a center of activity.

Group C: items 3, 6, 7, 10, 13, 16, 20.

Contrast items 3 and 6. Do you like a quiet or a talkative mate?

Contrast items 7 and 20. Which kind of life style would you like better?

Items 10, 13, 16. Tap your physical and parental instincts. The higher you scored, the more you want a mate who is relaxed and easy in these matters.

How Big Is Your Ego?

This test is designed to assess to what degree you see yourself as the center of your world and how predominant you are over others with whom you interact. Answer each item by circling one choice.

1. When four of you are sitting at the table for dinner
   (a) you like to be served first.
   (b) you like your mate to be served first.
   (c) you like your kids (or friends) to be served first.

2. When you and a stranger arrive at the same parking spot simultaneously
   (a) you let him take the spot.
   (b) you take the spot yourself.
   (c) you immediately look for another spot.

3. When you are tired in the morning
   (a) you ask your mate to get up first to prepare breakfast.
   (b) you get up first.
   (c) you get up with your mate at the same time.

4. When a new magazine arrives
   (a) you give it to someone else to read first.
   (b) you do not care who reads it first.
   (c) you insist on reading it first.

5. When standing in line to buy tickets
   (a) you do not care if someone cuts in line in front of you.
   (b) you do not let anyone cut in line in front of you.
   (c) you get annoyed if someone cuts in line, but you don't say anything.

6. When a piece of candy has been divided into a big and a small piece
   (a) you take the big piece for yourself.
   (b) you take the small piece for yourself.
   (c) you let the other person make the choice.

7. If you were to rank family members' importance in the upkeep of your home, it would be
   (a) self, mate, children.
   (b) mate, self, children.
   (c) mate, children, self.

8. When pouring drinks, in what order do you pour into whose glasses?
   (a) friend's, mate's, yours.
   (b) yours, mate's, friend's.
   (c) mate's, yours, friend's.

9. If your home were on fire
   (a) you would run out first to call for help.
   (b) you would take everybody out into the street.
   (c) you would run out with one child calling for help to rescue the rest.

10. If the phone rings and there are others in the house
   (a) you wait until someone answers it or may pick it up if you are nearest the phone.
   (b) you let it ring until someone else answers it.
   (c) you get up to answer it first.

Scoring:

Item	Choice	Points
1	a	3
	b	2
	c	1
2	a	2
	b	3
	c	1
3	a	3
	b	1
	c	2
4	a	1
	b	2
	c	3
5	a	1
	b	3
	c	2
6	a	3
	b	1
	c	2
7	a	3
	b	2
	c	1
8	a	1
	b	3
	c	2
9	a	3
	b	1
	c	2
10	a	2
	b	3
	c	1

Score: 10-16   Modest ego   17-22   Average ego   23-30   Inflated ego

The Dual Morality Standard Test/Judgment of Others	This test measures hypocrisy, the presence of which does not predict good relationships with people.
Assertiveness	A good relationship is based on both partners' confidence that their needs are being understood, and their rights not trampled on. Since no one can expect the existence in one's life of someone whose sole function is to try to anticipate and satisfy one's needs, proper assertiveness skills will ensure that you take care of your own needs when necessary. By taking this responsibility, you will avoid many situations wherein you blame the other person for "not knowing what I wanted, and not giving it to me."
Dating	The higher this score, the more comfortable you will feel in initiating relationships.
How Do You Feel About Authority?	A high score here indicates you are a "take charge" person — a good trait to possess for success in work relationships. However, a low score, indicating you are a conformist, will ensure that you are loved by most.
Attitude Toward Your Children	A high score here predicts success overall in relationships with others.
Relationship with Your Mate	This test gives you a direct measure of the quality of your relationship with your mate — the primary relationship in your life.
Color Test II	While this test is not included on the report card, it gives valuable information on your feelings toward the people you have selected to consider.
Who's Your Ideal Mate?	While this test cannot be scored for inclusion on your report card, it tells you what type of mate you would consider ideal.
How Big Is Your Ego?	The more egocentric you are, the greater the likelihood that your relationships will be one-sided and chaotic.

Test Results

As you review the report cards of John and Sheila Bowers below, you will quickly see why their marriage was so successful. In almost all areas they both score well on the tests predictive of a good relationship.

While no tests are ever foolproof, it would be good to consider the factors covered by these tests in trying to improve your personal relationships. If there is conflict in your relationship with your mate, have him or her take the tests as well. You should then have a clearer idea where the deficiencies are in each of you and can work on improving your interpersonal skills in a guided and intelligent way.

Report Card for Personal Relationships

Sheila Bowers, Wife

Tests	Low		Medium		High	
Dual Morality Standard Test/Judgment of Others	20	13	12	7	6 ✱	0
Assertiveness	15	25	26 ✱	35	36	45
Dating	12	20	21 ✱	29	30	36
How Do You Feel About Authority?	39	30	29	22	21 ✱	13
Attitude Toward Your Children	+	14"	14"	7"	7" ✱	0
Relationship with Your Mate	15	25	26	35	36 ✱	45
How Big Is Your Ego?	30	23	22	17	16 ✱	10

Report Card for Personal Relationships

John Bowers, Husband

Tests	Low		Medium		High	
Dual Morality Standard Test/Judgment of Others	20	13	12 ✱	7	6	0
Assertiveness	15	25	26	35	36 ✱	45
Dating	12	20	21	29	30 ✱	36
How Do You Feel About Authority?	39	30	29	22	21 ✱	13
Attitude Toward Your Children	+	14"	14" ✱	7"	7"	0
Relationship with Your Mate	15	25	26	35	36 ✱	45
How Big Is Your Ego?	30	23	22	17	16 ✱	10

Instructions: Go back to each of the tests included in this report card and transfer your score by placing an X on the score you obtained. Your overall standing will be indicated by where the majority of the X symbols are placed.

Report Card for Personal Relationships

Myself

Tests	Low		Medium		High	
Dual Morality Standard Test/Judgment of Others	20	13	12	7	6	0
Assertiveness	15	25	26	35	36	45
Dating	12	20	21	29	30	36
How Do You Feel About Authority?	39	30	29	22	21	13
Attitude Toward Your Children	+	14"	14"	7"	7"	0
Relationship with Your Mate	15	25	26	35	36	45
How Big Is Your Ego?	30	23	22	17	16	10

Report Card for Personal Relationships

Mate

Tests	Low		Medium		High	
Dual Morality Standard Test/Judgment of Others	20	13	12	7	6	0
Assertiveness	15	25	26	35	36	45
Dating	12	20	21	29	30	36
How Do You Feel About Authority?	39	30	29	22	21	13
Attitude Toward Your Children	+	14"	14"	7"	7"	0
Relationship with Your Mate	15	25	26	35	36	45
How Big Is Your Ego?	30	23	22	17	16	10

8 Are You Keeping Up With the Joneses?

Do you own an item with any of the following names on it: Gucci, Louis Vuitton, Fendi? Or do you brag about how much you love your ten-year old Volvo? If so, you can skip this entire chapter since you have already gone "Tilt" on the status-consciousness scale.

Status awareness is a far more important issue than people are usually willing to admit. On an individual basis, you can observe that people always strive to perform job tasks or engage in hobbies that give them high status. Frequently they will defer financial gains for status considerations. Your boss gives you a new title with more prestige and you decide you can wait a little longer for that raise after all. You are status conscious. You look for that new car and decide to buy a top-of-the-line model even though, deep in your heart, you know that a cheaper, less prestigious model would run just as well and save you a great deal of money. You are status conscious. Your concern about your daughter's fiancé leads you to ask questions about his background, the community in which he was raised, his father's occupation, how prestigious is the university from which he graduated, etc. You are status conscious. Your daughter's happiness depends mostly on how sensitive he is to her needs and she to his. And yet prestige and status issues preoccupy you.

Western society is not the only afflicted by the status-consciousness virus. Communist societies also stress status, perhaps even to a greater degree than democracies. The Russian ballerina or internationally famous athlete who brings prestige to the motherland gets the dacha in the country and the Zil limousine — not the hard-working physician who saves many lives in the course of his duties. Pecking orders exist in every society, including the animal kingdom, in which they were first described. Since people can be so preoccupied with their station in life and attempt with such zeal to improve their position on the status ladder, it is important for you to know just how much you are motivated and your behavior determined by these considerations. The tests in this chapter will enable you to evaluate your propensity to put status and prestige above all other considerations.

Don't be discouraged if your scores are low. Remember, status and substance are not synonymous.

Moral Values Test

This test is designed to assess your opinion about certain situations. Answer each item by circling the number which best represents your opinion.

	Not Important	Somewhat Important	Quite Important	Very Important
1. Is it important to make sure you have enough money for your child's education before you decide which car to buy for your work purposes?	1	2	3	4
2. It is important to help a hungry beggar before you yourself have your lunch?	1	2	3	4
3. Is it important to give up your own comfort for the sake of getting a sick person to the doctor?	1	2	3	4
4. Is it important to oppose a law you strongly disagree with?	1	2	3	4
5. Is it important to help an escaped prisoner from a horrible prison?	1	2	3	4
6. Is it important to be very honest in the world of business?	1	2	3	4
7. Is it important for a doctor to kill a fetus if it endangers the mother's life?	1	2	3	4
8. Was it important to confine all Japanese people in the U.S. during the war against Japan?	1	2	3	4
9. Is it important to stop publication of a newspaper that criticizes the government?	1	2	3	4
10. Is it important to curb unions of agricultural workers?	1	2	3	4
11. Is it important to let high school students do whatever they wish?	1	2	3	4
12. Is it important to know at least one person one dislikes?	1	2	3	4

Scoring: For questions 1, 2, 3, 4, 6, 7, tally the numbers you circled.

For questions 5, 8, 9, 10, 11, 12, reverse the order of the numbers (if you circled 1, score 4 points; change 2 to 3; 3 to 2; and 4 to 1). Tally and add to the above score.

Score:

12-24	Low range of moral values
25-36	Medium range of moral values
37-48	High range of moral values

How Do You Rate the Status Symbols of Others?

This test will tell you how you evaluate other people's success in life. Answer each statement by circling the number representing your opinion.

	Low Status	Medium Status	High Status
1. A man driving an expensive car	1	2	3
2. A woman living in a big house	1	2	3
3. A man with a doctorate in geography	1	2	3
4. A woman astronaut	1	2	3
5. A winner of an "Honesty in Business" contest	1	2	3
6. A woman with four happy children	1	2	3
7. A person who can eat in the best restaurants all he wishes	1	2	3
8. A person owning a purebred dog	1	2	3
9. A person whose hobby is going to the theater	1	2	3
10. A person with a steady job	1	2	3

Scoring: Tally the numbers you circled.

Score: 16-30   You believe that people who are rich, honest, and have a family and a hobby are basically successful people.

10-15   You don't believe that the above characteristics have much to do with success in life.

What Status Symbols Are Important to You?

This test indicates how you would see your status level in various situations. Answer each question by circling the number representing your feeling.

	Low Status	Medium Status	High Status
1. If I could go to restaurants not worrying about the cost	1	2	3
2. If I never lied again	1	2	3
3. If I were never unemployed	1	2	3
4. If I owned a racehorse	1	2	3
5. If I liked going to museums	1	2	3
6. If I had a university degree	1	2	3
7. If I owned an expensive diamond ring	1	2	3
8. If I were a pharmacist	1	2	3
9. If I won $20,000 in a lottery	1	2	3
10. If I had four happy children	1	2	3

Scoring: Tally the numbers you circled.

Score: 16-30   You feel that being rich, honest, and having a family and other interests make you a successful person.

          10-15   You don't believe that any of the above have much to do with success in life.

Now determine the difference score between your answers to this test and the preceding test. Subtract the lower number from the higher one in each pair, then total the difference scores. The pairs are:

Preceding Test	This Test
7	1
5	2
10	3
8	4
9	5
3	6
1	7
4	8
2	9
6	10

Difference score:

     0-15   There is no big difference between what you feel constitutes success for others and for yourself, with some variations.

   16-30   It seems you have a double status standard. One for yourself and one for others.

Self-Esteem Test

This test will show you how you see yourself as a person. Answer each question by checking either Yes or No.

                                             Yes   No

1. I'm pretty/handsome.
2. I am smarter than the average individual.
3. I learn fast.
4. I have a nice body.
5. I am healthy.
6. I enjoy sex.
7. I am friendly to most people.
8. I am a relaxed person.
9. Life treats me well.
10. People think highly of me.
11. I am successful in my occupation.
12. I am a satisfied person.

Scoring: Score 1 point for each No checked and 2 points for each Yes.

Score:	12-15	Low self-esteem. You don't think too much of yourself.
	16-19	Average self-esteem. Most people feel similarly about themselves.
	20-24	High self-esteem. You believe in yourself and feel good about yourself.

Etiquette Test

This test aims to establish your knowledge concerning norms and rules while interacting with others.

1. When setting the table for a formal dinner, in which direction in relation to the plate ought the knife to face? _____

2. What is the name of the article of clothing worn around the waist of a man in formal attire? _____

3. From which side of a seated guest should you pour the wine? _____

4. What color wine is to be served with fish? _____

5. What is meant by R.S.V.P. on wedding invitations? _____

6. On which side of a woman (in relation to the street) is a male escort supposed to walk? _____

7. The sommelier is consulted on (a) catering (b) the choice of wine (c) seating of guests (d) interior decorating _____

8. Should a dinner guest arrive with a bottle of wine for his host? _____

9. When should one kiss a woman's hand? _____

10. The consort of a monarch must walk how many paces behind? _____

11. Is it ever acceptable to eat chicken with your fingers? _____

12. Amy _____ is well known for her books on etiquette.

13. V.S.O.P. on a Cognac bottle means _____

14. A demitasse is used for _____

15. When breaking wind in a social setting, the appropriate remark should be:
    (a) "It sounds like the rain is approaching."
    (b) "I'm sorry, but I haven't been the same since they removed my colon."
    (c) "Did you also enjoy *Blazing Saddles?*"

Answers:

1. To the right facing in.
2. Cumberbund.
3. The right side.
4. White.
5. *Répondez s'il vous plait.*
6. Street side.

7. (b) the choice of wine.
8. No! the host most likely has already selected the wine.
9. You don't. One only gestures to kiss the hand.
10. Five paces.
11. Yes, but only after a knife and fork won't do the job and then only with one hand.
12. Vanderbilt.
13. Very superior old pale.
14. Coffee.
15. Subtract one point if you selected either (a), (b), or (c).

Scoring: Score 1 point for each correct answer.

Score: 1-5   Definitely a boor.
        5-10   You have a sensibility for "what's right."
Above   10   Private school trained.

What Do You Really Know About Status?

This test will tell you how much you know about how different occupations rank according to their socioeconomic level. Each profession is rated according to the average salary and social recognition the holder receives. Your task is to rank the occupations in each item from the highest status to the lowest.

1. (a) dentist (b) surveyor (c) nurse (d) flight attendant (e) schoolteacher

2. (a) author (b) computer programmer (c) auditor (d) librarian (e) religious worker

3. (a) office manager (b) janitor (c) toolmaker (d) miner (e) commercial pilot

4. (a) fisherman (b) taxi driver (c) plumber (d) funeral director (e) gov't inspector

Answers:

1. (a) (e) (b) (c) (d)
2. (c) (b) (a) (d) (e)
3. (e) (a) (c) (d) (b)
4. (d) (e) (c) (b) (a)

Scoring: Score 4 points for each correct answer, or 2 points for a partially correct answer (at least three of the five professions in correct order).

Score: 0-5   Poor knowledge of occupational status
        6-11   Average knowledge of occupational status
        12-16   Good knowledge of occupational status

Interpretation of Report Card Scores

Moral Values Test	Generally, it can be expected that a person whose score is high will be concerned about others and what they think. Lowscorers are not concerned with anything beyond themselves.
Status Symbols of Others/Status Symbols Important to You	These two tests assess how much your opinions of yourself and others are influenced by what you think society holds to be right and proper.
Self-Esteem Test	As you hold up the mirror to admire yourself (not a bad thing to do once in a while), you judge your value according to social standards, to a degree. This test tells you how much weight you give to these criteria as reflected in your self-concept.
Etiquette Test	The higher this score, the more conscious you are about being socially correct.
What Do You Really Know About Status?	Your awareness of the status value of certain occupations reveals how status oriented you are.

Test Results

I own a pedigreed dog, drive a Cadillac, and have my hair cut by an expensive hair stylist. Care to see my Status Consciousness Report Card? Just see below.

Now fill out your report card and see if you can be more of an effete snob than I am.

Report Card for Status Consciousness

Sidney Lecker, Psychiatrist, Author, and Effete Snob

Tests	Low		Medium		High	
Moral Values Test	12	24	25	36	37 ✳	48
Status Symbols of Others	10	16	17	23	24 ✳	30
Status Symbols Important to You	10	16	17	23	24 ✳	30
Self-Esteem Test	12	15	16	19	20 ✳	24
Etiquette Test	1	5	6	10	11 ✳	15
Status Awareness	0	5	6	11	12 ✳	16

Instructions: Go back to each of the tests included in this report card and transfer your score by placing an X on the score you obtained. Your overall standing will be indicated by where the majority of the X symbols are placed.

Report Card for Status Consciousness

Tests	Low		Medium		High	
Moral Values Test	12	24	25	36	37	48
Status Symbols of Others	10	16	17	23	24	30
Status Symbols Important to You	10	16	17	23	24	30
Self-Esteem Test	12	15	16	19	20	24
Etiquette Test	1	5	6	10	11	15
Status Awareness	0	5	6	11	12	16

9 How's It Going?

Have you ever known anyone in the mid-life crisis? That is the time of life in which men and women may impulsively decide to leave their jobs, get a divorce, change careers, or have an affair. Why do otherwise rational people so recklessly abandon an ostensibly satisfying life? Usually, it is because they have never really bothered to take an inventory of the various aspects of their life in order to evaluate whether or not they are satisfied with their overall life style. People tend to become entrenched in the work, relationships, and recreational activities that they have become accustomed to. Despite changing needs and growing obsolescence of their lives, rarely do they pick up a scalpel and perform the delicate surgery necessary to transform the way in which they live. Suddenly, in the mid-life crisis, things explode and come apart in all directions. Usually the results of the mid-life crisis are massive changes based on disillusionment with oneself and one's life style. However, too often the change is unsatisfactory because it is the result of an evaluation made too suddenly. What would be much more productive and far less traumatic would be a periodic inventory and evaluation of the way in which one lives throughout the entire adult life cycle.

This chapter will give you some ideas and guidance as to how to conduct such an inventory. It is not meant to be an exhaustive review of your life style, since no questionnaire that the author could design would be able to predict the specifics of each person's unique life. But after completing the tests in this chapter, you will be able to understand what type of questions to ask yourself in evaluating your life style. Then, by consulting the information in Chapter Thirteen, you can learn to design tests that will be tailor-made to evaluate the full range of activities that make up your daily life.

Be reflective and sincere when taking the tests, and above all, don't rush. The results of this evaluation are far too important to be hastily considered.

Your Job

This test is designed to help you assess your feelings concerning various aspects of your job. Answer each question by putting a checkmark in the appropriate column.

	I would like to change it	Not sure	I would not like to change it
1. What I feel generally about my work . . .			
2. My salary . . .			
3. The time I have to start working . . .			
4. The time I finish working . . .			
5. The actual work I am doing . . .			
6. The people I work with . . .			
7. The room I work in . . .			
8. The tools (aids) I use . . .			
9. My boss's attitude . . .			
10. Fringe benefits that come with my job . . .			
11. Vacation or time off I get . . .			
12. The location of my work (in city or town) . . .			
13. The physical conditions of my work (noise, space, lighting) . . .			
14. Repetitiveness of work . . .			
15. Recognition I get for doing this work . . .			

Scoring: Tally the checkmarks in each column. Multiply the number in the first column by 3, in the second column by 2, and in the third column by 1. Now total the three scores.

Score: 15-25   You are probably quite satisfied in your job.

        26-35   You are uneasy about some things, but do not know exactly what to try to change.

        36-45   You should either quit or try hard to change your work conditions. You don't seem to like them much.

The Meaning of Success at Work

This test is designed to help you establish what is important to you at work. What is it in your work situation that makes you feel successful at what you do or would make you feel that way in the future? There is no score for this test, just a list of work related issues. To answer, place a checkmark in the appropriate columns. After you finish, pay particular attention to the items you designated as very important and contemplate whether or not you have figured out how to deal with them.

	Unimportant	Somewhat Important	Very Important
1. Your salary in comparison to the boss's salary.			
2. Your salary in comparison to the salary of another worker who is equal to you in rank.			
3. The way your boss treats you.			
4. Other workers' respect for you.			
5. What society thinks of your job.			
6. What your family thinks of your job.			
7. The opportunities for advancement.			
8. Whether or not you feel you can be creative.			
9. The degree to which your job fits your personality characteristics.			
10. The degree to which you're willing to put in extra hours when needed.			
11. The purpose of your work (the service or benefits others gain from your work).			
12. Your rank (level of responsibility) at work.			

The Meaning of Leisure Activity

This test is designed to help you determine whether you are satisfied with your leisure activities. There is no score for this test. It's purpose is to show you what you deem important in your activities and encourage you to think of ways to make more satisfying use of your leisure time. Place a checkmark in the column representing the degree of importance you attribute to each item.

	Unimportant	Somewhat Important	Very Important
1. Amount of leisure time . . .			
2. Whether you spend it with a friend or alone . . .			
3. Physical surroundings (indoors or outdoors) . . .			
4. Whether it is relaxing . . .			
5. Whether you obtain an "energy release" . . .			
6. If sports, what it does for your physical fitness . . .			

	Unimportant	Somewhat Important	Very Important

7. If arts, satisfaction in creativity . . .

8. The fact that it helps to pass the time . . .

9. Learning new things through leisure activity . . .

10. Offers social opportunities . . .

11. Helps you to forget work and chores . . .

12. The fact that everybody does something besides work and chores . . .

Fantasy Test

This test should help you determine to what degree you fantasize about certain matters in your life. Answer each question with an honest word or two. Scoring follows the next test.

1. What kind of job would you like to have? _____

2. What salary would satisfy your needs? _____

3. How large would you like your house or apartment to be? _____

4. How many children would you like to have? _____

5. How long a vacation would you like to take each year? _____

6. How many good friends would you like to have? _____

7. How many times a week would you like to go to the movies or theater? _____

8. Would you like to be married? _____

9. Would you like to be in excellent physical condition? _____

10. Would you like to study something? _____

11. Would you like to have an interesting hobby? _____

12. Would you like to get rid of headaches? _____

Reality Test

This test is designed to gather some information about various matters in your life. Answer each question honestly with a word or two.

1. How many good friends do you have? _____
2. How many times a week do you go to the movies or theater? _____
3. Are you married? _____
4. In what physical condition are you? _____
5. Are you studying something? _____
6. Do you have some interesting hobbies? _____
7. Do you suffer headaches often? _____
8. What field do you work in? _____
9. What is your salary? _____
10. How large is your home? _____
11. How many children do you have? _____
12. How long is your yearly vacation? _____

Scoring: The reality test and the fantasy test have to be interpreted by you. Compare your answers to each of the following pairs and note whether or not there is a discrepancy. In most cases, the greater the discrepancy between fantasy and reality the more a person uses fantasy to compensate for situations which are not to his liking. If there are no discrepancies in your life, you can consider yourself happier than most people. Score one point for every set of questions in which fantasy and reality are far apart.

Reality Test	Fantasy Test
1	6
2	7
3	8
4	9
5	10
6	11
7	12
8	1
9	2
10	3
11	4
12	5

Satisfaction with Life Style

This test is designed to help you determine how happy you are with your present life style. Answer each item by circling one of the three numbers.

		Unhappy	Neutral	Happy
1.	The amount of money I spend on clothing.	1	2	3
2.	The number of times I eat out.	1	2	3
3.	The places I go to with my mate.	1	2	3
4.	The intellectual stimulation I receive.	1	2	3
5.	The kind of friends I have.	1	2	3
6.	The kind of sex life I have.	1	2	3
7.	The kind of home I have.	1	2	3
8.	The kind of entertainment I experience.	1	2	3
9.	The kind of vacations I take.	1	2	3
10.	The kind of job I have.	1	2	3
11.	The financial security I have.	1	2	3
12.	My leisure activities.	1	2	3
13.	My physical condition.	1	2	3
14.	The way I care for myself.	1	2	3
15.	The amount of respect I get from others.	1	2	3

Scoring: Tally the numbers you chose as answers.

Score: 15-25   You seem to be unhappy with your life style. Check which aspects you could improve.

26-35   You are basically satisfied but there is room for improvement.

36-45   You are happy with how life is treating you.

How Do You Think Others See You?

This test is designed to help you determine to what degree you feel other people respect you for who you are and what you do. When answering the items, think about people who are important in your life and their opinion of you, then circle the appropriate number.

	Not Respected Very Much	Moderately Respected	Respected Very Much
1. The way I talk.	1	2	3
2. The way I dress.	1	2	3
3. My manners.	1	2	3
4. My body.	1	2	3
5. My sexual ability.	1	2	3
6. The issues which interest me.	1	2	3
7. My political opinions.	1	2	3
8. My work.	1	2	3
9. The money I make.	1	2	3
10. My share in the household.	1	2	3
11. My education.	1	2	3
12. My hobbies.	1	2	3
13. My assertiveness.	1	2	3
14. My sociability.	1	2	3
15. My self-confidence.	1	2	3
16. My intelligence.	1	2	3
17. My creativity.	1	2	3
18. My *joie de vivre*.	1	2	3
19. My optimism/pessimism.	1	2	3
20. My understanding of others.	1	2	3

Scoring: Tally the numbers you circled.

Score: 20-33 Low social esteem
34-47 Average social esteem
48-60 High social esteem. People respect many aspects in you.

Interpretation of Report Card Scores

Your Job   This test gives you a direct measure of job satisfaction.

The Meaning of Success at Work

While this test is not scorable for inclusion on the report card. It can help you decide which aspects of work reward or frustrate you.

Fantasy/Reality Test and Satisfaction with Life Style

These tests give you a good idea of how close you now are to your real goals and hidden dreams. The closer the better, in terms of satisfaction with your life style.

How Do You Think Others See You?

High scorers on this test believe that they are "someone special" — a good feeling for anyone to have and a measure of satisfaction with one's life style.

Test Results

Paul came into my office seeking divorce counseling. He was convinced that his marriage was at an end and wanted to know how to implement a divorce with minimum trauma for all family members. As we discussed his life style, it became apparent that his dissatisfaction arose from his work, where he felt in a rut, and from increasing boredom with his recreational activities. His Satisfaction with Life Style report card clearly revealed that he needed a job change far more than a divorce.

Fill in your report card and assess how satisfied you are with your current life style.

Report Card for Satisfaction with Life Style

Paul Shapiro, Stockbroker

Tests	Low	Medium	High
Your Job	45 ✱ 36	35 ¦ 26	25 ¦ 15
Fantasy/Reality Test	12 ✱ 9	8 ¦ 5	4 ¦ 0
Satisfaction with Life Style	15 ✱ 25	26 ¦ 35	36 ¦ 45
How Do You Think Others See You?	20 ¦ 33	34 ✱ 47	48 ¦ 60

Instructions: Go back to each of the tests included in this report card and transfer your score by placing an X on the score you obtained. Your overall standing will be indicated by where the majority of the X symbols are placed.

Report Card for Satisfaction with Life Style

Tests	Low	Medium	High
Your Job	45 ¦ 36	35 ¦ 26	25 ¦ 15
Fantasy/Reality Test	12 ¦ 9	8 ¦ 5	4 ¦ 0
Satisfaction with Life Style	15 ¦ 25	26 ¦ 35	36 ¦ 45
How Do You Think Others See You?	20 ¦ 33	34 ¦ 47	48 ¦ 60

10 How Do You Want It to Go?

"I am bored."

"I am really plateaued in my job."

"Even the things that used to satisfy me a few years ago have become very unpalatable."

These are not the complaints of a severely depressed individual. They are dilemmas tha arise in the lives of most people as they grow and mature, and their needs and interests shift.

Everyone needs to have a certain degree of excitement in life and, in most cases, this means that life must continually change in a variety of ways. Who would want to stay in the same job for a lifetime? Who would want one's marriage to remain in a consistent pattern with predictable activities for years on end? Why would anybody want to take a vacation at the same resort year after year? Despite your satisfaction with the way things are today, undoubtedly your present activities will become stale and therefore boring at some future point. You should begin to assess your changing preferences right now in order to predict the type of life style you will have to construct if you are to be happy in the future.

The tests in this chapter will give you guidance in evaluating your major preferences in a variety of areas. There is no scoring system or report card at the end of this chapter, for an important reason. Tests, if they are to be valid at all, should be based on measuring observable behavior. Since these tests are designed to elucidate preferences for a future life style, they have no bearing on your present behavior.

The test results can guide you in selecting certain activities with which to experiment. You may decide to sample a new hobby. Possibly, you will consider a modification in your job or career path based on the information that the tests provide. However, these assessments should be viewed as "experimentation," not as "final conclusions."

Your Future Play

This test will assess how you spend your leisure time and what areas of interest seem to be most rewarding to you. Read each statement and check either Yes or No.

	Yes	No
1. In my free time I often finish some things which I didn't manage to do during my work hours.		
2. Most of my leisure time is spent on things completely unrelated to my work.		

3. When I'm at home, I spend much of my time fixing things, an activity which isn't my hobby.

4. Most often, I spend my free time reading a book or a newspaper.

5. Most often, I spend my free time watching TV.

6. I prefer spending my free time at home.

7. I prefer spending my free time engaging in active sports.

8. I could say that I have a hobby in which I'm actively involved.

9. Usually, after a free weekend, I feel quite bored.

10. I get great pleasure out of puttering around the house.

11. Most often, I like to spend my free time with people I like.

12. I would like to spend my free time going to the movies.

13. I like going to a museum when I'm off work.

14. I spend my leisure time most often with the people I work with.

15. I spend my free time doing something creative (building something, artwork, crafts).

16. I enjoy spending my free time alone.

17. I don't have a hobby because it would demand too much time.

18. I spend time with a group of friends who have the same ideas about how to spend their free time.

19. I like my job so much that I wouldn't mind working overtime.

20. Usually I need someone to give me a good idea for how to spend my weekends.

21. I like (or would like) to spend time caring for houseplants.

Scoring: As there are an infinite number of activities a person could engage in during his or her leisure hours, scoring this test would not tell you whether you're a "movie-goer," a "stamp collector," or "swinger" in your free time. Your answers should make you think of more general trends concerning your leisure.

How "hooked" are you on your job? Do you have an existence outside it? Consult your answers to items 1, 2, 14, and 19.

Can you enjoy your free time by yourself? Or do you need a "buddy" for enjoying your free time? Consult your answers to items 11, 16, 18, and 20.

Do you like to spend more free time inside your home or away from it? Related items: 3, 6, 7, and 10.

Do you feel you have something which could be called a hobby? Items 8, 9, 15 and 17.

Is your involvement in your leisure activities of an active or passive nature? Items 4, 5, 12, 13, and 21.

Arts/Science/Economics Aptitude

Aptitude in a particular area is often reflected in the knowledge one accumulates relative to that area. The following questions deal with well-known facts in science, music, art, and economics.

1. Franz Liszt composed

   (a) *Don Sancho* (b) *Die Fledermaus* (c) *Hungarian Rhapsodies* (d) *The Merry Widow*

2. The metallic element which is the lightest of all solid bodies is

   (a) nickel (b) lithium (c) cadmiun (d) mercury

3. He developed the vaccination for smallpox.

   (a) Louis Pasteur (b) Edward Jenner (c) Alexander Fleming (d) Jonas Salk

4. Which one of the following was not composed by Stravinsky?

   (a) *The Firebird* (b) *Petrouchka* (c) *The Rite of Spring* (d) *Islamey*

5. The color of light with the longest wavelength is

   (a) red (b) yellow (c) green (d) blue

6. The Sherman Anti-Trust Act became law in

   (a) 1914 (b) 1924 (c) 1890 (d) 1939

7. "That government is best which governs least" was a notable quote of

   (a) John Maynard Keynes (b) Adam Smith (c) Paul Samuelson (d) James Earl Carter

8. Which of the following was not a member of the French Impressionist School?

   (a) Paul Delvaux (b) Claude Monet (c) Edgar Degas (d) Pierre Renoir

9. A sculptor, he is known for the *Burghers of Calais*, *The Thinker*, *The Kiss*, and *Balzac*.

   (a) Auguste Rodin (b) Henry Moore (c) Georg Kolbe (d) Arnaldo Pomodoro

10. He was an English satirical painter and engraver.

    (a) Edward Hopper (b) Joshua Reynolds (c) Philip Steer (d) William Hogarth

11. $T = Tm + (To - Tm) e^{-A+}$ is

    (a) a mole fraction (b) a hypergeometric distribution (c) the Nernst formula
    (d) Newton's Law of Cooling

12. The *Hungarian Dances* were composed by

    (a) Johannes Brahms (b) Robert Schumann (c) Piotr Tchaikovsky (d) Lawrence Welk

13. A nematode is a

    (a) roundworm (b) carboniferous plant (c) one-celled animal (d) species of fish

14. John D. Rockefeller built an empire in the

    (a) real estate business (b) automobile business (c) oil business (d) fur business

15. Which of the following was not a Rodgers and Hammerstein collaboration?

    (a) *The Girl Friend* (b) *Oklahoma!* (c) *South Pacific* (d) *The King and I*

16. A potassium-sodium pump is a necessary conceptualization for

    (a) coagulation (b) nerve impulse transmission (c) respiration (d) digestion

17. Greenbacks were first issued in
    (a) 1776 (b) 1875 (c) 1862 (d) 1917

18. An art movement aiming to express the imagination as revealed in dreams is called
    (a) dadaism (b) expressionism (c) surrealism (d) impressionism

19. The selling of stock you have not yet purchased is called
    (a) a take (b) an option (c) a bid (d) selling short

20. While beset with growing deafness, he wrote some of his greatest music.
    (a) Wagner (b) Beethoven (c) Tchaikovsky (d) Sullivan

Answers:

1. (c) 2. (b) 3. (b) 4. (d) 5. (a) 6. (c) 7. (b) 8. (a) 9. (a)
10. (d) 11. (d) 12. (a) 13. (a) 14. (c) 15. (a) 16. (b) 17. (c)
18. (c) 19. (d) 20. (b)

Science	Music	Art	Economics
2) _____	1) _____	5) _____	6) _____
3) _____	4) _____	8) _____	7) _____
11) _____	12) _____	9) _____	14) _____
13) _____	15) _____	10) _____	17) _____
16) _____	20) _____	18) _____	19) _____

Scoring: Give yourself one point for each correct answer. By comparing your totals on each area, you can assess your relative strengths and weaknesses.

Technical Aptitude

In this test you can find out how well you recognize objects and parts which are commonplace in our society. View each picture for 10 seconds and write down what it is.

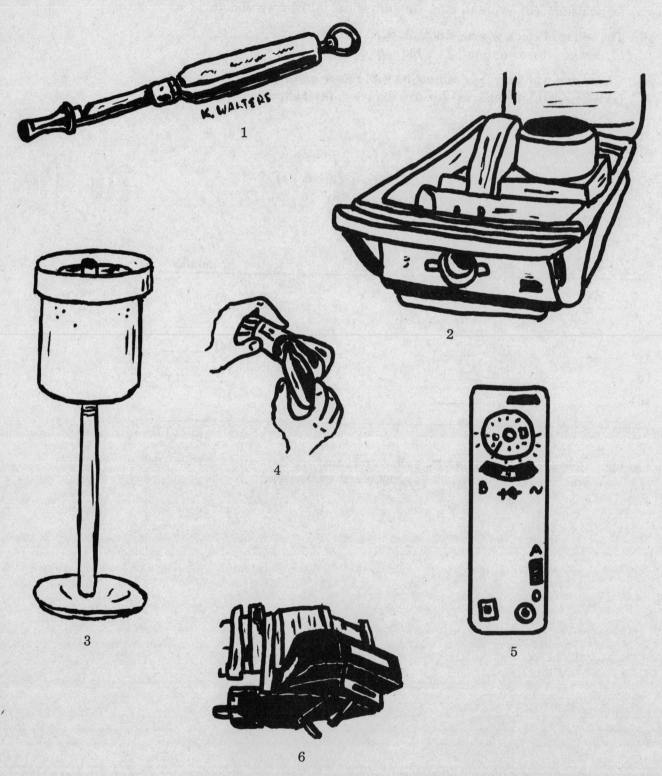

1

2

3

4

5

6

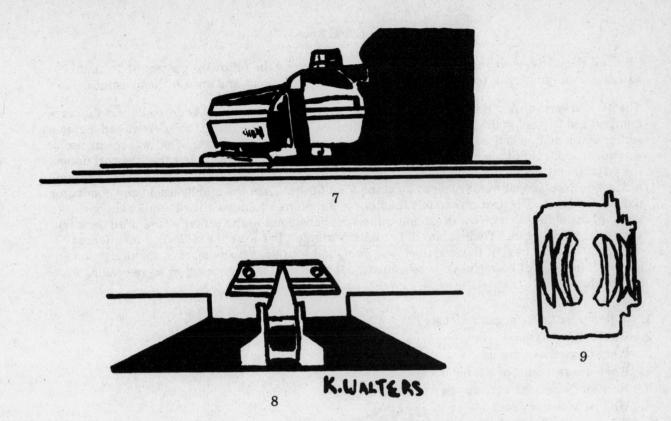

7

8

K. WALTERS

9

10

Answers:

1. Dog whistle
2. Vacuum cleaner
3. Percolator insert
4. CO_2 charger
5. Electronic flash
6. Hi-fi cartridge
7. Front ski binding
8. Typewriter ribbon guide
9. Camera lens elements
10. Hi-fi speakers

Scoring: Score 1 point for each correct answer.

Score: 1-3   Not very observant of technical detail

4-6   Average recognition

7-10   Very observant of technical detail

Reading Level and Speed

This test demands speed and concentration. You are to read the following passage in 1 minute, and as soon as you finish (or the minute is over) cover the passage and answer the questions.

The sea was very stormy that night. The fifteen hundred persons on the *Andromeda* and the seven hundred and fifteen on the *Rigoletto* were all thinking of the same thing: their crews had announced earlier that a million-and-one-half-ton iceberg had been sighted in the area. What was so worrisome was not that the tip of the iceberg loomed three hundred feet into the air, but that the part under the water might span a few miles in each direction. Everybody had finished his Sunday night dinner an hour ago and all were trying to keep the food down. Even the middle-aged band conductor did not feel well. The dancers had left the floor and preferred to nurse their brandies and gins. Some of the ladies went below deck, and those who had cabins in the center or the third deck felt somewhat more secure. Their cabins didn't have portholes, but were the closest to the lifeboat stations. Captain Grey, of the lead liner, was going to his bridge. As he reached the bridge someone handed him a pair of powerful Zeiss binoculars. He took it all in at once: they were heading for a bluish-white wall.

1. Where were the safer cabins located?
2. Where was the captain going?
3. What time of day was it?
4. What was the name of the big boat?
5. How many persons were on the smaller boat?
6. Who went below deck?
7. What was the name of the smaller boat?
8. What was the danger ahead?
9. Why were some cabins safer than others?
10. How many persons were on the big boat?
11. What age was the musician?
12. Which make were the binoculars?
13. Which drinks did most people drink?
14. What was the captain's name?
15. How much did the object weigh?

Scoring: Check your answers against the text. Score 1 point for each correct answer.

Score: 0-5   Poor reading comprehension

             6-10   Average reading comprehension

           11-15   Good reading comprehension. (Do you read enough to satisfy your intellect? Don't neglect reading for pleasure, since this skill comes so easy to you).

11 What Is Your S.Q. (Sex Quotient)?

How many times have you been "turned on" by an anonymous voice at the other end of the telephone line, intrigued by the inflections of the voice and its timbre? Haven't you had many experiences in which people with just average physical attractiveness got under your skin because of the depth of their understanding of your feelings and a mysterious and exciting quality in their personality? There are many constituents to sexual attractiveness that go beyond appearance and sexual performance criteria.

The tests in this chapter will reveal your sexuality quotient, or SQ. The purpose of the tests is to enable you to evaluate your sexual profile, thus giving you direction as to where you must improve in order to be a more appealing sexual partner. You and your sexual partner should both take the tests and then discuss the results together. Improving your sexuality is a process best accomplished by being both teacher and student to your sexual partner.

Repeat the tests after a period of several months. If you put to use the information derived from these tests, you will most probably find an improvement in your SQ score.

Sexual IQ

This test is designed to assess your knowledge of sexual response. Answer each item by circling the correct choice.

1. In the quiescent state, the clitoris
    (a) is engorged with blood   (b) retracts   (c) hangs neutrally   (d) is emptied of blood

2. In the quiescent state, the penis is
    (a) flaccid   (b) erect   (c) engorged with blood   (d) bloodless

3. In the highly aroused state, the clitoris
    (a) hangs vertically   (b) is emptied of blood   (c) is erect horizontally
    (d) rotates and retracts

4. In the highly aroused state, the testicles
    (a) ascend   (b) descend   (c) rotate   (d) tremble

5. During orgasm, the vaginal muscles contract with a
    (a) .15/second rhythm   (b) .26/second rhythm   (c) .17/second rhythm
    (d) .8/ second rhythm

6. During orgasm, the muscles of the penis contract with a
    (a) .17/second rhythm   (b) .8/second rhythm   (c) .15/second rhythm
    (d) .26/second rhythm

7. After orgasm, the clitoris returns to its normal position in
    (a) 5-10 seconds   (b) 10-20 seconds   (c) 20-30 seconds   (d) 30-40 seconds

8. After cessation of orgasmic contractions, the small lips of the vagina lose their deep red color in
    (a) 10-15 seconds   (b) 30-40 seconds   (c) 60-80 seconds   (d) 90-120 seconds

9. Once the penis has become flaccid, after orgasm, it is normal not to be able to regain an erection for a few hours if you are:
    (a) of adolescent age   (b) over 20 years old   (c) over 40 years old   (d) over 50 years old

10. Once penile erection has been attained, normally this state of excitement can be maintained
    (a) only for a relatively short time, less than 5 minutes   (b) for a relatively long period of time, over a half hour   (c) for several seconds   (d) 16 hours

Answers:

1.	(c)	6.	(b)
2.	(a)	7.	(a)
3.	(d)	8.	(a)
4.	(a)	9.	(d)
5.	(d)	10.	(b)

Scoring: Score 1 point for each correct answer.

Score: 0-3   Poor sexual IQ

   4-7   Good sexual IQ

   8-10   Very sexually oriented

Sexual MQ (Misconception Quotient)

This test is designed to establish the degree of sexual misconception you have. Answer the following items as either true or false.

1.	Having one testicle makes you sterile.	T	F
2.	There are several million sperm in each ejaculation.	T	F
3.	Homosexuals can't have intercourse with females.	T	F
4.	The normal penis size when flaccid is six inches long.	T	F
5.	Abundant pubic hair is a sign of fertility.	T	F
6.	The size of a man's testicles is related to his virility.	T	F
7.	A female can reach extravaginal orgasm.	T	F
8.	An ejaculation can be inhibited by squeezing under the tip of the penis.	T	F
9.	Masturbation causes genital cancer.	T	F
10.	Oral sex can cause dental caries.	T	F
11.	Homosexual fantasies are quite common.	T	F
12.	Sexual behavior begins at a pre-adolescent age.	T	F
13.	Big men usually have a big penis.	T	F
14.	The average male can maintain an erection for six hours.	T	F
15.	Most people in their twenties have masturbation experiences.	T	F
16.	No female creature kills after having had sex with her mate.	T	F

Answers:

1.	F		9.	F	
2.	T		10.	F	
3.	F		11.	T	
4.	F		12.	T	
5.	F		13.	F	
6.	F		14.	F	
7.	T		15.	T	
8.	T		16.	F	

Scoring: Score 1 point for each correct answer.

Score: 0.5   High level of sexual misconceptions

6-10   Medium level of sexual misconceptions

11-16   Low level of sexual misconceptions

Are You Romantic?

This test is designed to help you determine how much of a romantic you are. Indicate your preferences by circling the appropriate number for each item.

A. When I invite someone for dinner I do it
    (1) by phone   (2) by letter   (3) with a flower or small gift   (4) by messenger

B. A show of affection between strangers should be done through
    (1) a handshake   (2) flowers   (3) a kiss   (4) a wedding ring

C. An appropriate place for the first dinner date is
    (1) a pizzeria   (2) McDonald's   (3) own apartment   (4) quiet restaurant

D. The most romantic object on the table when having a date home for dinner is
    (1) flowers   (2) wine   (3) candles   (4) turkey

E. Which composer would you prefer for background music?
    (1) John Philip Sousa   (2) Carl Orff   (3) Rachmaninoff   (4) Shifrin

F. What color rose will you give your female date?
    (1) yellow   (2) red   (3) white   (4) pink

G. Which of the following peoples are thought to be the most romantic?
    (1) Japanese   (2) Mexicans   (3) Swedes   (4) Italians

H. Which opera would you rate as most romantic?
    (1) *Falstaff*   (2) *La Boheme*   (3) *Die Fiedermaus*   (4) *Rigoletto*

I. Which place would you say is most romantic for a loving pair?
    (1) top of the Empire State Building   (2) seashore at dusk   (3) Niagara Falls
    (4) O'Hare Airport

Answers:
    A.   (3)
    B.   (2)
    C.   (4)
    D.   (3)
    E.   (3)
    F.   (2)
    G.   (4)
    H.   (3)
    I.   (2)

Scoring: Score 1 point for each correct answer.

Score: 0-3   Not much romance in your soul

           4-6   You have a certain romantic flair

           7-9   Highly romantic

Sexual Experience Questionnaire

This questionnaire is designed to help you organize your thoughts about your past and present sexual experiences. Answering the questions may prove helpful in facilitating discussion of intimate matters with your mate or lover. Or, if you have some unresolved difficulty in your sexual relations, you will find it easier, upon answering these questions in writing, to talk to a sex counselor concerning the problem.

1. At what age did you start to date?
2. What kind of petting did you engage in?
3. How did you feel about these activities?
4. Did you engage in premarital intercourse?
5. Are you orgasmic?
6. Do you have any problems with erection, or premature ejaculation?
7. If you suffer from premature ejaculation, at what point in the sex act does this happen?
8. What feelings accompany intercourse?
9. What form of contraception do you use?
10. Have you ever had difficulty achieving penetration? Is the penis unable to penetrate due to tightness of vaginal muscles?
11. Do you have sexual fantasies?
12. Do you masturbate? Accompanied by what fantasies?
13. Have you had sexual encounters with a person of the same sex? How do you feel about this?
14. Have you had any unpleasant sexual encounters with a stranger? With a family member? How do you feel about this?
15. How do you feel about the following (in terms of positive or negative feelings): masturbation; oral sex; intercourse; erotic literature; pronographic movies; sexual fantasies?

Interpretation of Report Card Scores

Sexual IQ	This test measures your specific knowledge on sexual matters. The higher your score, the more sexually oriented you are.
Sexual MQ	A high score indicates solid knowledge on sexual matters. A low score reveals stereotyped beliefs, as well as misinformation.
Are You a Romantic?	A high score on this test reveals that you are a good lover, not just a competent performer. There is a difference between making love and having sex. Check your score here to see which you do.

Test Results

The value of this group of tests is self-evident. Consider the report card of a girl I met at Club Méditerranée during my bachelor days. Do you wonder why I took up sailing for the balance of my vacation after our first encounter? Could you handle that kind of SQ?

Now fill in your report card and have your mate do the same. By repeating these tests after several months, you will be able to judge your improvement as a sexual partner.

Report Card for Sexuality Quotient

The Girl I Met at Club Méditerranée

Tests	Low		Medium		High	
Sexual IQ	0	3	4	6	7 ✖	10
Sexual MQ	0	5	6	10	11 ✖	16
Are You a Romantic?	0	3	4	6	7 ✖	9

Instructions: Go back to each of the tests included in this report card and transfer your score by placing an X on the score you obtained. Your overall standing will be indicated by where the majority of the X symbols are placed.

Report Card for Sexuality Quotient

Myself

Tests	Low		Medium		High	
Sexual IQ	0	3	4	6	7	10
Sexual MQ	0	5	6	10	11	16
Are You a Romantic?	0	3	4	6	7	9

Report Card for Sexuality Quotient

My Mate

Tests	Low		Medium		High	
Sexual IQ	0	3	4	6	7	10
Sexual MQ	0	5	6	10	11	16
Are You a Romantic?	0	3	4	6	7	9

12 Test Your Stress

As a doctor, if I were to pick out one factor that would be most predictive of your future health, it would be the way in which you respond to stress. Research has shown that the Type A personality is far more vulnerable to heart attack based on that personality factor — a particular way of coping with stress — than heredity, diet, or any other single factor. The Type A personality is one who constantly feels under some kind of pressure. There is always the need to rate one's self numerically, and then to compare one's self with others. If Type A personalities were taking these tests, for example, they would not be content with finding out about themselves or even hoping to improve in an individual way. They would need someone else to compare their "scores" with, and the need to "improve" said ratings would be competitive. In fact, the Type A personality is never satisfied with his or her own performance. He or she could always have done "better" or "more" if only there had been "more time" or some other change in circumstance. This is a compulsive, driven personality, who lives constantly with stress. This is not to say that stress alone determines whether or not you will be healthy or ill, but the way in which you mobilize your resources to cope is crucial in terms of your vulnerability to disease.

There are certain tests in this chapter that can help you to define your specific way of dealing with life stresses. Once you have scored your report card, you will be able to identify areas of vulnerability to stress.

Remember, tests are themselves stress-producing, and so you will perform best if you manage to keep your stress within a comfortable range.

Stress Checklist

Check Yes or No depending on whether any of the following events describe your circumstances over the last two years.

		Yes	No
1.	Began a new job		
2.	Death in the family		
3.	Change in financial condition		
4.	Divorce		
5.	Change in size of family		
6.	Separation		
7.	Outstanding achievement		
8.	Serious illness		
9.	Problems in relationships with other sex		
10.	Retirement		
11.	Change in job		
12.	Death of spouse		
13.	Money problems		
14.	Marriage		

Scoring: For questions 2, 4, 6, 10, 12, and 14 multiply the number of Yes answers by three. Score 1 point for each remaining Yes.

A score over 20 is very high, and you run a risk of developing a major psychiatric or medical illness within the next two years. A score between 10 and 20 also involves a risk, suggesting you have experienced considerable change in the recent past and face the prospect of stress affecting your physical and psychological functioning.

Stress-Prone Test

Consider how you respond to each of the following situations and place a check at the appropriate point on the continuum.

1. Traffic jams
    I tolerate $\qquad$ 1   2   3   4   5   Drive me crazy

2. Competition
    Like $\qquad$ 1   2   3   4   5   Dislike

3. Relaxation
    Easy for me $\qquad$ 1   2   3   4   5   Difficult for me

4. Deadlines
    Must never be 1   2   3   4   5   Are flexible
    missed

5. Impatient
    Not me $\qquad$ 1   2   3   4   5   Me

6. Work
    Important $\qquad$ 1   2   3   4   5   Unimportant

7. Energetic
    Not me $\qquad$ 1   2   3   4   5   Describes me

8. Being on time
    Important $\qquad$ 1   2   3   4   5   Unimportant

9. Tolerant
    Describes me $\qquad$ 1   2   3   4   5   Not me

10. Irritated
    Often $\qquad$ 1   2   3   4   5   Never

Scoring: For questions 1, 3, 5, 7, 9, add up the checks that fall between points 4 and 5. For questions 2, 4, 6, 8, 10, add up the checks that fall between points 1 and 2.

If your score is above 5, it is likely you are a Type A individual. The higher the score, the greater this likelihood.

Drug Use

This test is designed to assess your level of drug use. Answer each question by circling the appropriate choice.

1. I smoke cigarettes
   (a) not at all (b) less than one pack a day (c) more than one pack a day

2. I drink alcoholic beverages
   (a) never (b) only at parties (c) more often than (b)

3. I smoke pot (or hash)
   (a) never (b) once a month (c) several times a week

4. I take tranquilizers
   (a) not at all (b) on rare occasions (c) every day

5. I take amphetamines
   (a) never (b) once in a long while (c) quite regularly

6. I take prescription drugs
   (a) almost never (b) a few times a year (c) quite regularly

7. I use LSD
   (a) never (b) seldom (c) regularly

8. I take drugs in order to escape daily troubles
   (a) never (b) sometimes (c) often

9. I take drugs to a "loss of control" state
   (a) never (b) sometimes (c) often

10. "Drugs are man's best friend."
    (a) Disagree (b) Don't know (c) Agree

Scoring: Score 1 point for each (a) you circled; 2 points for each (b); 3 points for each (c).

Score: 10-16   Low level of drug use
          17-22   Medium level of drug use
          23-30   High level of drug use

Self-punishment Test

This test is designed to assess how much you directly or indirectly punish yourself. Answer each question by checking either Yes or No.

Yes   No

1. Do you smoke cigarettes?
2. Do you drink alcohol regularly?
3. Do you take unnecessary medication (or drugs)?
4. Have you had three or more operations?
5. Do you put yourself down in interactions with your mate?
6. Do you put yourself down in interactions with your friends?
7. Do you put yourself down in interactions with your kids?
8. Do you sometimes drive a car while intoxicated?
9. Do you sometimes express your anger by driving your car faster?
10. Do you sometimes express your anger by hitting the wall with your fist?
11. Do you sometimes express your anger by putting your fist through a door or window?
12. Do you bite your fingernails when you're nervous?
13. Do you pull on your hair when you're anxious?
14. Do you dig your fingernails into your arms or hands when you're upset?
15. Do you eat a lot to calm yourself down?

Scoring: Score 1 point for each Yes answer.

Score: 1-5   Mildly self-punishing
          6-10   Self-punishing to an unhealthy degree
          11-15   Dangerously self-punishing

Accident-Prone Test

This test is designed to determine to what degree you have a tendency to be involved in accidents or mishaps. Answer each item by checking either Yes or No.

	Yes	No
1. Do you cut your fingers often?		
2. Do you stumble on the sidewalk often?		
3. Do you often step on other people's feet?		
4. Do you drop your groceries often?		
5. Do you often drop a pen or pencil?		
6. Do you break dishes often?		
7. Do you sometimes break a match when trying to light a cigarette?		
8. Do things happen to fall on you (e.g., lamps, books)?		
9. Have you been involved in a traffic accident?		
10. Were you "almost" hit by a car?		
11. Have you forgotten to shut the stove off before going out?		
12. Have you ever fallen down stairs?		
13. Do you burn yourself often?		
14. Do you scratch your car fenders a lot?		

Scoring: Score 1 point for each Yes answer.

Score: 1-4   Probably just a bit absent-minded rather than accident-prone

5-8   Definite tendency to accident proneness

9-14   Highly accident-prone

Body Responses

This test is designed to tell you to what degree your body functions respond to specific situations. For each item circle the number which most adequately represents the changes you're aware of. If you don't know, circle no. 1.

Situation A: You are alone at a party where you don't know many people.

	Not at all				Extremely
Heart beats faster	1	2	3	4	5
Perspire	1	2	3	4	5
Need to urinate	1	2	3	4	5
Mouth gets dry	1	2	3	4	5
Voice quivers	1	2	3	4	5
Hands shake	1	2	3	4	5
Stomach muscles contract (butterflies)	1	2	3	4	5
Feel dizzy	1	2	3	4	5

Situation B: A policeman gives you a traffic ticket.

Heart beats faster	1	2	3	4	5
Perspire	1	2	3	4	5
Need to urinate	1	2	3	4	5
Mouth gets dry	1	2	3	4	5
Voice quivers	1	2	3	4	5
Hands shake	1	2	3	4	5
Stomach muscles contract	1	2	3	4	5
Feel dizzy	1	2	3	4	5

Situation C: You're introduced to a new date.

Heart beats faster	1	2	3	4	5
Perspire	1	2	3	4	5
Need to urinate	1	2	3	4	5
Mouth gets dry	1	2	3	4	5
Voice quivers	1	2	3	4	5
Hands shake	1	2	3	4	5
Stomach muscles contract	1	2	3	4	5
Feel dizzy	1	2	3	4	5

Situation D: You just received very bad news in a letter.

Heart beats faster	1	2	3	4	5
Perspire	1	2	3	4	5
Need to urinate	1	2	3	4	5
Mouth gets dry	1	2	3	4	5
Voice quivers	1	2	3	4	5
Hands shake	1	2	3	4	5
Stomach muscles contract	1	2	3	4	5
Feel dizzy	1	2	3	4	5

Situation E: You're waiting for your turn at the dentist's.

Heart beats faster	1	2	3	4	5
Perspire	1	2	3	4	5
Need to urinate	1	2	3	4	5
Mouth gets dry	1	2	3	4	5
Voice quivers	1	2	3	4	5
Hands shake	1	2	3	4	5
Stomach muscles contract	1	2	3	4	5
Feel dizzy	1	2	3	4	5

Situation F: You are waiting to enter for a job interview.

Heart beats faster	1	2	3	4	5
Perspire	1	2	3	4	5
Need to urinate	1	2	3	4	5
Mouth gets dry	1	2	3	4	5
Voice quivers	1	2	3	4	5
Hands shake	1	2	3	4	5
Stomach muscles contract	1	2	3	4	5
Feel dizzy	1	2	3	4	5

Situation G: You are about to go on a roller coaster.

Heart beats faster	1	2	3	4	5
Perspire	1	2	3	4	5
Need to urinate	1	2	3	4	5
Mouth gets dry	1	2	3	4	5
Voice quivers	1	2	3	4	5
Hands shake	1	2	3	4	5
Stomach muscles contract	1	2	3	4	5
Feel dizzy	1	2	3	4	5

Situation H: A stranger approaches you on the street at night.

Heart beats faster	1	2	3	4	5
Perspire	1	2	3	4	5
Need to urinate	1	2	3	4	5
Mouth gets dry	1	2	3	4	5
Voice quivers	1	2	3	4	5
Hands shake	1	2	3	4	5
Stomach muscles contract	1	2	3	4	5
Feel dizzy	1	2	3	4	5

Scoring: Tally the number of points you scored for the 64 answers you circled.

Score:

64-100   You're either unreactive physiologically to most situations or you lack awareness as to how your body responds to what you hear, see, feel, and think.

101-250   You fall into the wide average range of bodily responsiveness. You're also quite aware of what's going on inside you.

251-320   You would seem to be very reactive to many situations, a bit anxious. You may benefit from relaxing yourself before entering into a wide variety of everyday situations.

Knowing and Controlling Your Body

This test will show you how familiar you are with, and how well you can control, a specific physiological response — your heart rate. Follow the described steps, but stop immediately if you feel any discomfort.

1. (a) Estimate your heart rate at this moment. Write down your estimate. Then count your pulse (beats per minute) by placing your index finger on the inside of your wrist.

   (b) Walk from where you are sitting to the door and back, twice at a fast pace. Estimate your pulse, then take the actual rate as described above.

   (c) Perform ten knee bends (squatting down and standing up). If you feel weak, stop at once. Estimate your pulse, then count the actual rate.

2. (a) Measure your pulse. Write it down. Sit in a chair. Concentrate on your heartbeat. Repeat silently to yourself: "Be calm, relax . . . I'm calming down . . . I'm relaxing." Do this for two minutes. Measure pulse. Write it down. Repeat procedure for another three minutes. Measure pulse again.

   (b) Walk around the room a few times, then lie on a bed repeating the procedure described in 2 (a).

Scoring: 1 (a): If you estimated within 10 beats per minute (b.p.m.): 2 points

   If you estimated within 15 b.p.m.: 1 point

   If you estimated within 20 or more b.p.m.: 0 points

   1 (b): Same scoring as above

   1 (c): Same scoring as above

   2 (a): If you reduced your pulse by 8 b.p.m. after 2 minutes: 4 points

   If you reduced your pulse by 6 b.p.m. after 2 minutes: 2 points

   If you reduced your pulse by 4 b.p.m. after 2 minutes: 1 point

   If you reduced your pulse by 8 b.p.m. after 3 minutes: 3 points

   If you reduced your pulse by 6 b.p.m. after 3 minutes: 1 point

   If you reduced your pulse by 4 b.p.m. after 3 minutes: 0 points

   2 (b): Same scoring as in 2 (a).

For part 1: If you scored higher than 4 points, you demonstrate an accurate perception of your heart rate functioning. If you scored less than 4, you guessed incorrectly, but you could learn to estimate correctly.

For part 2: Score: 0-4 Poor control over your pulse rate

   5-9 Average control over your pulse rate

   10-14 Good control over your pulse rate

The better the control you demonstrate, the more likely it is that you would be able to deal with situations which cause you unpleasant excitement.

Enter your score in part 2 of the report card for this section.

Testing Your Fear and Anxiety

This test is designed to assess whether you suffer from fear and anxiety in various life situations. Answer each question by checking either Yes or No.

		Yes	No
1.	Are you squeamish with insects?		
2.	Are you afraid of snakes?		
3.	Are you afraid of dogs?		
4.	Do you get dizzy when you are in open areas (i.e., a large parking lot)?		
5.	Do you get tense in an elevator?		
6.	Do you get dizzy when looking down from a high place?		
7.	Have you ever canceled a plane trip because of fear of flying?		
8.	Have you been unable to swallow food due to tension?		
9.	Have you experienced increased heart rate during takeoff in a plane?		
10.	Are you afraid to go out alone in the dark?		
11.	Have you been scared to stay home alone at night?		
12.	Do you feel tense while crossing a bridge?		
13.	Do you feel tense when you swim in deep water?		
14.	Are you afraid of germs?		
15.	Did you ever get so nervous before having to give a talk that you had to cancel it?		
16.	Are you afraid of tests?		

Scoring: Score 1 point for each Yes answer.

Score:
- 1-5   Low level of fear and anxiety
- 6-10   Medium level of fear and anxiety
- 11-16   High level of fear and anxiety

Is Your Body Telling You Something?

This test is designed to establish your level of physical complaints. Answer each question by checking either Yes or No.

		Yes	No

1. Do you suffer often from headaches which seem to have no clear preceding event?
2. Do you suffer from migraine?
3. Do you suffer from unexplainable toothaches?
4. Do you suffer from a chronic colic condition?
5. Do you have frequent digestion difficulties?
6. Do you have an active ulcer?
7. Do you have any asthmatic conditions?
8. Do you suffer from hypertension?
9. Do you experience palpitations often?
10. Do your hands shake?
11. Do you experience sweating spells?
12. Do you experience spells of feeling very cold?
13. Have you seen a doctor more than three times this past year?
14. Have you been operated on more than three times to date?

Scoring: Score 1 point for each Yes answer.

Score:
1-2   Good psychological and physical state.

3-6   Somewhat elevated level of physical complaints. Probably psychologically based.

7-14   High level of physical complaints. Psychological basis should be explored.

Interpretation of Report Card Results

Stress Checklist	Generally the more change you face in your life, the more stress you experience.
Stress-Prone Test	High scorers on this test are apt to respond to situations in a way that will increase harmful stress.
Drug Use and Self-punishment Tests	Individuals usually have similar scores on these two tests. The use of drugs is a sign of high stress combined with a poor coping response. Self-punishment also reveals unfortunate lack of competence under crisis conditions.
Accident-Prone Test	People under heavy stress are known to be more accident prone. They can't concentrate well and their coordination is poorer while under stress.
Body Responses	You should evaluate two aspects of your physical reactions to stress: how much of a reaction you undergo while tense (rapid heartbeat etc.), and how rapidly these functions return to normal. While some people react severely to stress with racing pulse, sweaty palms, etc., they have learned to recover quickly so as to minimize the duration of their stress reaction. Biofeedback and meditation help severe reactors learn to recover quickly from stress reactions of their bodies. If you scored high on this test, you might consider taking up one of these stress-control techniques.
Knowing and Controlling Your Body	If you scored high on this test of controlling your body functions, you should be quite able to control your stress reactions.
Testing Your Fear and Anxiety	The more fearful you are, the more stress-prone you will be.
Is Your Body Telling You Something?	This is a test to detect hypochondriasis, an exaggerated concern with one's health associated with stress-prone individuals.

154

Test Results

A man sought consultation with his physician because he felt he could not get enough air into his lungs — believing himself to have a respiratory condition of some sort. The astute doctor noticed how much the man's blood pressure fluctuated from one moment to the next and how much time pressure he seemed to be under (constantly glancing at his watch), and diagnosed the condition as hyperventilation syndrome. The man was an extremely stress-prone individual, and highly susceptible to future mental and physical illness. Rather than give him tranquilizers, the doctor recommended biofeedback training. Within six weeks all the symptoms were gone. By simply learning to quiet down his stress responses, this man was able to reduce his vulnerability to serious illness.

Review this man's Report Card for Vulnerability to Stress to see why he was suffering so much and then fill out your own. Do you think you should learn better ways to relax and reduce your stress?

Report Card for Vulnerability to Stress
A Man with Hyperventilation Syndrome

Tests	Low		Medium		High	
Stress Checklist	0	10	11	20	21 ✖	+
Stress-Prone Test	0	3	4	6	7 ✖	+
Drug Use	10 ✖	16	17	22	23	30
Self-punishment Test	1	5	6	10	11 ✖	15
Accident-Prone Test	1	4	5 ✖	8	9	14
Body Responses	64	100	101	250	251 ✖	320
Knowing and Controlling Your Body	14	10	9	5	4 ✖	0
Testing Your Fear and Anxiety	1	5	6	10	11 ✖	16
Is Your Body Telling You Something?	1	2	3	6	7 ✖	14

Instructions: Go back to each of the tests included in this report card and transfer your score by placing an X on the score you obtained. Your overall standing will be indicated by where the majority of the X symbols are placed.

Report Card for Vulnerability to Stress

Tests	Low		Medium		High	
Stress Checklist	0	10	11	20	21	+
Stress-Prone Test	0	3	4	6	7	+
Drug Use	10	16	17	22	23	30
Self-punishment Test	1	5	6	10	11	15
Accident-Prone Test	1	4	5	8	9	14
Body Responses	64	100	101	250	251	320
Knowing and Controlling Your Body	14	10	9	5	4	0
Testing Your Fear and Anxiety	1	5	6	10	11	16
Is Your Body Telling You Something?	1	2	3	6	7	14

13 A Quiz on Test Building

Now that you have taken the tests in this book to rate yourself in the various important areas of your life, how would you like to become the tester instead of the testee? It might be quite useful to you to know how to design a test that would evaluate the performance of your spouse, your doctor, your lawyer, your bank manager, your boyfriend or girl friend, or any other important person in your life. It is really not so difficult to construct a test that is tailor-made to assess whatever functions or roles you wish to evaluate. There are several basic steps to test construction that you must know:

1. First you must define which specific function you wish to evaluate. Is it your doctor's bedside manner? Or your husband's sensitivity to your needs? Or the quality of advice you receive from your lawyer? These and many other aspects of your life can be evaluated by designing a specific test to do so.

2. After you have selected what it is that you wish to test, you must analyze that function of the person's behavior. For example, if you wish to measure your spouse's sensitivity to your needs, you must define specific behaviors that reveal this capacity. And so, you might decide to use:

(a) The time spent with you each day in discussing your needs.

(b) The number of positive actions taken by your spouse as a result of that discussion.

(c) The number of times your spouse has forgotten an important need in a given period of time, for example, in one month.

By translating this abstract notion — your spouse's sensitivity to your needs — into specific behavior that can be measured, you have taken the first important step in constructing a test that will assess that particular function.

3. Now you must decide to what use you wish to put the information derived from the test. There are several ways of deriving information with respect to your spouse's sensitivity to your needs. For example, you may simply want to have a True or False answer for each question. Let us say you have constructed a ten-item test, with a score of 1 point for each "True" answer. This type of test is quite useful in evaluating the overall changes in your spouse's sensitivity. For example, if the test result shows three Trues today and improves to seven Trues in three months, you know that your spouse is making progress in learning to be sensitive to your needs.

A different type of test can be constructed, assessing the same behavior but giving quantitative information rather than an absolute "True" or "False" answer. For example, you might construct a list of questions that measure degree of response to your needs, such as:

1. My spouse spends an adequate amount of time
   discussing and trying to understand my needs.   A   a   d   D

2. My spouse forgets or neglects my needs no
   more than average.   A   a   d   D

   Where A = strongly agree; a = mildly agree; d = mildly disagree; and D = strongly disagree.

This type of questionnaire not only allows you to cover the same material as the True/False type of questionnaire but also give you an estimate of *how* true or false each statement is. Since obviously there may be differences of degree between how responsive your spouse is on each of these items, this type of questionnaire allows you to evaluate behavior in a more precise way. The questions can be answered in this four-category way, or you can set up a rating scale with numerals, such as:

1. My spouse spends an adequate amount of time discussing and trying to understand my needs.
   -5 -4 -3 -2 -1 0 +1 +2 +3 +4 +5

2. My spouse forgets or neglects my needs no more than average.
   -5 -4 -3 -2 -1 0 +1 +2 +3 +4 +5

Where -5 is strong disagreement or the lowest possible score, and +5 is the best score.

Using this scale, you can then add up the total score for an overall rating of your spouse's sensitivity, and can measure progress in each specific item as your spouse's sensitivity either improves or deteriorates over the ensuing months. This type of questionnaire, therefore, is a more sensitive way of evaluating each function measured on the test as well as tracking the progress of your relationship.

1. My spouse is attentive   -5 -4 -3 -2 -1 0 +1 +2 +3 +4 +5

2. I look forward to being alone with my spouse   -5 -4 -3 -2 -1 0 +1 +2 +3 +4 +5

(Add up all scores to give an overall total.)

+1 (total score)

Another way of using tests is to evaluate the differences between people in the way they perceive important issues. Take for example the same issue, "sensitivity to your needs." You can design a test that is administered to husband and wife in which they each separately answer the same questions. You would discern their conflict by assessing the questions on which they differed most significantly. In so doing, you will have given them important insight and direction as to how to rectify their problems with regard to sensitivity to each other's needs. Such a questionnaire would be constructed as follows:

1. It is important for husbands and wives to spend a significant period of time on a weekly basis discussing each other's needs.   A a d D

2. When your spouse forgets an important event in your life such as your birthday, he or she should be severely chastised and made to feel guilty.   A a d D

Now it is time to build your own test in order to confirm what you have learned about the value and uses of tests. In the form on page 158 there are places for ten questions. Pick out a function that you wish to measure, for example the development of morality in your child. You might ask:

1. My child makes an attempt to tell the truth on most occasions.
2. Whenever my child considers doing something to someone else, he or she asks the question, "How would I feel if that was done to me?"

By addressing questions like this you can begin to assess your child's moral development. Of course, the more extensive the questions, the more accurately you will be able to assess an issue. That is why in many tests there are hundreds of questions asked in order to be sure that all facets of the issue are covered.

	-5	-4	-3	-2	-1	0	+1	+2	+3	+4	+5

1.

2.

3.

4.

5.

6.

7.

8.

9.

10.

A Quiz on Test Building

In the following test, check the items according to whether they are true or false.

	True	False

1. In constructing a test, you must select behavior that can be rated in some fashion.

2. A True/False format allows you to measure specific functions to a precise degree.

3. Tests are an excellent way of developing objective criteria that can be used to measure a person's progress in a specific function or capacity.

4. In tests given to two individuals in order to reveal differences in their attitudes on specific issues, their scores will indicate which person is superior in specific functional areas.

5. Once you have given a person a test and derived a score or rating for him in a particular function, you can predict how he will act with respect to that function under all given circumstances.

6. The more questions you include on a test, the more confusing and unreliable the test is.

7. Tests are excellent ways of comparing people's attitudes about specific issues.

8. Tests can be used as a measure of progress if you test an individual over a period of time and compare the scores (provided you don't repeat the test so frequently that he or she memorizes the correct answers).

9. Once you have taken a test and scored poorly, you ought to avoid that area of functioning in your life since you are destined for failure and frustration.

10. Tests which measure such aspects as mood and personality can give you information just as useful as that which you can derive from consulting a psychologist or psychiatrist.

Answers:

1.	T	6.	F
2.	F	7.	T
3.	T	8.	T
4.	F	9.	F
5.	F	10.	F

Scoring: Score 1 point for each correct answer.

8-10   You are quite knowledgeable about tests, their construction and purposes.

4-7   Your knowledge about tests could use some improvement. It might be a good idea to reread this chapter.

0-3   Take up golf or tennis and stop worrying about your test results.

Test Blank to Reveal Areas of Conflict Between Individuals

1.   A   a   d   D
2.   A   a   d   D
3.   A   a   d   D
4.   A   a   d   D
5.   A   a   d   D
6.   A   a   d   D
7.   A   a   d   D
8.   A   a   d   D
9.   A   a   d   D
10.   A   a   d   D

Where A = strongly agree; a = mildly agree; d = mildly disagree; and D = strongly disagree.

Test for a Specific Function, Such as My Spouse's Sensitivity to My Needs

1.   -5 -4 -3 -2 -1   0 +1 +2 +3 +4 +5
2.   -5 -4 -3 -2 -1   0 +1 +2 +3 +4 +5
3.   -5 -4 -3 -2 -1   0 +1 +2 +3 +4 +5
4.   -5 -4 -3 -2 -1   0 +1 +2 +3 +4 +5
5.   -5 -4 -3 -2 -1   0 +1 +2 +3 +4 +5
6.   -5 -4 -3 -2 -1   0 +1 +2 +3 +4 +5
7.   -5 -4 -3 -2 -1   0 +1 +2 +3 +4 +5
8.   -5 -4 -3 -2 -1   0 +1 +2 +3 +4 +5
9.   -5 -4 -3 -2 -1   0 +1 +2 +3 +4 +5
10.   -5 -4 -3 -2 -1   0 +1 +2 +3 +4 +5

Total Score _____